THE ART OF
CONSCIOUS
CONVERSATIONS

THE ART OF
CONSCIOUS
CONVERSATIONS

TRANSFORMING HOW WE
TALK, LISTEN, AND INTERACT

CHUCK WISNER

Berrett–Koehler Publishers, Inc.

Berrett-Koehler Publishers, Inc.
1333 Broadway, Suite 1000
Oakland, CA 94612-1921
Tel: (510) 817-2277
Fax: (510) 817-2278
www.bkconnection.com

ORDERING INFORMATION
Quantity sales. Special discounts are available on quantity purchases by corporations, associations, and others. For details, contact the "Special Sales Department" at the Berrett-Koehler address above.
Individual sales. Berrett-Koehler publications are available through most bookstores. They can also be ordered directly from Berrett-Koehler: Tel: (800) 929-2929; Fax: (802) 864-7626; *www.bkconnection.com*.
Orders for college textbook / course adoption use. Please contact Berrett-Koehler: Tel: (800) 929-2929; Fax: (802) 864-7626.

Distributed to the U.S. trade and internationally by Penguin Random House Publisher Services.

Berrett-Koehler and the BK logo are registered trademarks of Berrett-Koehler Publishers, Inc.

Printed in the United States of America.

Berrett-Koehler books are printed on long-lasting acid-free paper. When it is available, we choose paper that has been manufactured by environmentally responsible processes. These may include using trees grown in sustainable forests, incorporating recycled paper, minimizing chlorine in bleaching, or recycling the energy produced at the paper mill.

Library of Congress Cataloging-in-Publication Data.
Names: Wisner, Chuck, author.
Title: The art of conscious conversations : transforming how we talk,
    listen, and interact / Chuck Wisner.
Description: First edition. | Oakland, CA : Berrett-Koehler
    Publishers,Inc., [2023] | Includes bibliographical references and index.
Identifiers: LCCN 2022014868 (print) | LCCN 2022014869 (ebook) | ISBN
    9781523003266 (paperback) | ISBN 9781523003273 (pdf) | ISBN
    9781523003280 (epub) | ISBN 9781523003303
Subjects: LCSH: Interpersonal communication. | Interpersonal relations. |
    Communication in organizations.
Classification: LCC BF637.C45 W57 2023 (print) | LCC BF637.C45 (ebook) |
    DDC 153.6—dc23/eng/20220617
LC record available at https://lccn.loc.gov/2022014868
LC ebook record available at https://lccn.loc.gov/2022014869

First Edition
30 29 28 27 26 25 24 23 22   10 9 8 7 6 5 4 3 2 1

Book design and production: Happenstance Type-O-Rama
Cover design: David Ter-Avanesyan

To my wife, Kata,
for her love, friendship,
and kind heart,

and

Ben and Sam, my sons,
for testing and teaching me
so I could do and be better.

I love you all to pieces!

CONTENTS

Part I

STORYTELLING CONVERSATIONS
Your Stories Are Not the Truth

Part II

COLLABORATIVE CONVERSATIONS
Seek to Understand and Absorb Other Perspectives

PREFACE

Twenty-five years ago I worked as an associate at a mid-size firm in Cambridge, Massachusetts, where one of the partners was struggling with an alcohol problem. His behavior became increasingly toxic for the firm's leadership, our employees, and our clients. As leaders, we were frustrated and stuck in negativity, which magnified the dysfunction. We had no idea how to navigate these troubled waters.

At that time, I was immersed in Stephen Covey's book *The 7 Habits of Highly Effective People*. I had learned just enough from the book to know that we could no longer avoid the issue. We reached out for help, and after burning through a few ineffective consultants, the universe delivered a gem of a business coach named Linda Reid. Her experience, knowledge, empathy, and fresh eyes allowed her to assess the personal and business dynamics at our firm. She introduced us to practical tools that gave us new insights and skills for managing the situation. We hit some rough patches, but eventually we made changes by having more conscious conversations and agreed on how to move forward.

I was captivated by Linda's work. I wondered, *How did she do that? What does she know that I don't?* Other than Covey's book, I had no formal training in management or leadership, so her work seemed magical. I was humbled, inspired, and insatiably thirsty to learn more.

My long-held interests in philosophy, psychology, and spirituality aligned with what I learned from Linda. Inspired, and after four years of re-education and retooling, I began a new career in leadership, advising and coaching, focused on the power of language and conversations. I hope that, in these pages, I've bottled some of the "magic" that Linda and other teachers taught me and that I have cultivated over the last thirty years. It is now my privilege to share it with you and welcome you to the path of Conscious Conversations—a lifelong journey.

INTRODUCTION
Waking Up in Conversations

A bend in the road is not the end of the road. . . .
Unless you fail to make the turn.

—HELEN KELLER

As a young architect, I had a front-row seat for many conflicts in the building industry. The arguments were ubiquitous: architects versus engineers, engineers versus contractors, neighbors versus developers, and town officials versus owners. Given the big egos, the hardened positions, and the high stakes, it probably shouldn't have been surprising that so many of those conversations didn't go well.

One cold and snowy winter morning in a dank unfinished first-floor space, the construction project manager, a colleague named Seth, and I were facilitating a meeting to discuss the schedule and the monthly spend for the multimillion-dollar project. The building's owner ordered his representative, Kevin, to kick some ass in the meeting, making it clear that he didn't trust the contractor. Joe, the owner of the construction company, and his son were no fans of the owner or Kevin. Before the meeting, Seth and I accessed the dollar request and the budget. We planned to update the schedule and approve 80 percent of the payment request. During the meeting, Kevin kept interjecting, pushing for more concessions. He argued that the lack of progress meant that the $150,000 requisition wasn't earned. Joe and his son were furious. Without the full payment, they couldn't pay their subcontractors, and the project would come to a screeching halt.

Joe accused Kevin of being his boss's lackey, and Kevin told Joe that he and his son were incompetent. Emotions heated up and before Seth and I could cool things down, Joe's son leaped across the table and attacked Kevin. Seth and I managed to break up the fight, then we told Joe and his son to leave the site. After I got back to the office and calmed down, I started thinking about the insanity of the meeting. That room had been full of smart people with a common goal, yet they had still come to blows. Each person in the meeting had good intentions, but they also came with their own agendas, concerns, and rationales.

We have all experienced discouraging and stressful interactions like this one. Some are less dramatic, but others are completely chaotic. It's usually easy to walk away and hope to avoid these situations in the future, but that doesn't help us do better next time.

The Art of Conscious Conversations is an attempt to detangle the confusing web of daily conversations. Over time, as I worked with my clients using the concepts in this book, I often heard them say, "Why didn't I learn these concepts in elementary school? Life would have been much easier." Or, "This is hard work but it will definitely make me a better leader." Or, "I've never really paid attention to how judgmental I am."

We live in conversations like fish live in water. Just as fish swim in waters unaware, we thoughtlessly engage in conversations. Most of the time, we don't think about the thoughts or the words beneath the surface of our emotions, and we end up talking and listening on autopilot. One minute we're in heaven with our morning coffee and toast, and the next minute we're miserable because a text message from the boss sends us into a tizzy. In a flash, we wonder how to manage an impossibly demanding boss, and we wish it were time for our evening drink. And we talk to ourselves, our minds chattering away, saying things like, *If I don't get there on time, I'm totally screwed! Can it be six o'clock already? Will traffic be awful today? After work, I'm going to give Josh a piece of my mind.* And we talk to other people, saying such things as, "Where have you been hiding out?" And, "How can they vote for that man?" We get stressed and emotionally triggered, and we wonder how conversations can go so wacky. Often we aren't sure why things go wrong, and many of us don't have the tools to improve conversations or our relationships.

This book is a practical guide for learning about and thoughtfully reflecting on conversations and avoiding the common pitfalls that cause our relationships and work to go sideways. When we learn about the chemistry of cooking, we learn to cook better. When we know the rules of chess, we see a chessboard with new eyes. If we spent a year with the Inuit in the Arctic, immersing ourselves in their language and learning their many names for *snow,* we would never again see or experience snow in the same way. The same can be said of conversations. In this book, we explore the DNA of conversations so we can discover and appreciate the power and generative nature of language. We will gain a basic understanding of how and why our inner and outer conversations work (and don't work).

Our conversations—at home, at work, or in public—can be sources of pleasure and a stepping stone toward success, or they can cause us pain and lead us to failure. Because conversations are so vital to achieving our goals and so easily trip us up, they are due for a fresh look.

The great thinkers and teachers of the philosophy of language and linguistics have written much about communication and relationships, but their works tend to be daunting, challenging to comprehend, and not easily accessible. Their books are dense and are on the bookshelves of universities—here and abroad—or their programs are esoteric. In writing this book, I hoped to turn heady theories and philosophies into easily understandable concepts and provide the reader with tools that are enlightening and practical.

I have been refining the art of conscious conversations with my wife, kids, friends, and colleagues for the last twenty-five years. I have also been blessed to work with hundreds of clients who used the tools of this book to transform their conversations.

One of my clients, Jamie, and I got together to catch up over a drink after a year of not seeing one another. After we caught up on his work, Jamie asked me an intriguing question, "There are so many tools and practices that have been enormously helpful to me at home and work, but I'm having trouble understanding how they all fit together. Is there a way to connect the dots and organize them all?" In that moment, I didn't have an answer, but his question stuck with me for months. I wondered how I could structure and organize it all so that it was easier to understand and apply. On a beach walk with my wife months later, the answer found me. The many tools and complexity Jamie was wondering about could be organized by four fundamental types of conversations that I learned when studying with Julio Olilla, Rafael Echeverria, and Lesley Pollitt at the Newfield Institute, the first credited coaching program in the United States. That aha moment was the seed that became this book.

Four conversations—storytelling, collaborative, creative, and commitment—provide the structure for this book and help us connect the dots.

The Storytelling Conversation: Your Stories Are Not the Truth
Storytelling conversations consist of the stories we believe and tell ourselves and others. They define us in many ways and determine how we show up in the world. This part explores the hidden wisdom of our unspoken narratives and the complex, confounding relationships among our emotions, facts, and opinions.

The Collaborative Conversation: Seek to Understand and Absorb Other Perspectives
In this conversation, our individual stories intermingle with others' stories, surfacing divergent perspectives. In the collaborative conversation, we learn how to absorb opposing positions, change our own perceptions, lower our defenses, and transform our listening. We work with advocacy and inquiry to improve our conversational skills and to get smart with others.

The Creative Conversation: Trust Your Intuition

The creative conversation opens our minds and hearts to new insights. Through it, we explore the integration of the rational left hemisphere and the creative right hemisphere of our brains. The practices include learning to listen to our intuitions, to generate new ideas, and to value synchronicity with others. More present and open-minded, we're better prepared to see, hear, and act on opportunities that cross our path.

The Commitment Conversation: Don't Make Promises You Can't Keep

Commitment conversations are where the action is. Every day, we exchange inconsequential and weighty promises with others. From doing the dishes to signing a major contract, the promises we make to one another are the foundation of our coordination with others. Our agreements determine who does what, when, how, where, and why. They are how we get things done. The tools in Part IV help us make smarter decisions and mindful commitments that build trust.

The four conversations are distinct but also complementary. We can experience all four types in a flash, or we may need to focus on one more than another. Together they provide an endless supply of material to work with.

This book isn't a promise of new-age bliss, and no particular dogma or belief is required to have more conscious conversations. You only need a dogged and courageous determination to take a fresh look at your interactions with your bosses, friends, and loved ones—and with yourself.

My hope is that the concepts and practices will guide the reader to have more conscious conversations, satisfying relationships, and professional success. It is possible to live with less stress and more ease, one conversation at a time.

PRACTICES

Whatever your sport, practice improves your game. The practices of each chapter offer different reflections, insights, and everyday practical tools to improve your conversational game.

When you begin your exploration, try to observe yourself and your conversations objectively, with curiosity, and with less self-judgment. Start a notebook and write down your observations and thoughts. Noticing and noting rewires our brains' familiar, stressful communication patterns, allowing us to reconsider our conversations.

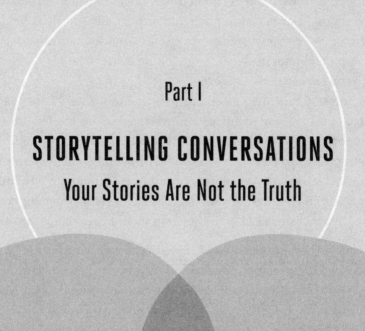

Part I

STORYTELLING CONVERSATIONS
Your Stories Are Not the Truth

A Note: Why Start with Storytelling?

When we use the word *conversation*, we generally think of dialogue with others. We tend not to think about the often-ignored, private thoughts that bounce around in our heads—sometimes called "the committee." But we really should include them in a discussion about conversations because our inner thoughts create and reflect the stories we believe and live by. Those private thoughts—whether conscious or unconscious— are the stories we believe and the bedrock of our communication.

Stories aren't inert. They contain truths and falsehoods and persuasive powers that can change minds, relationships, and decisions. I start by exploring our personal stories because you and your stories are the common denominator in every interaction, no matter who you're speaking with and no matter the context.

Chapters 1, 2, and 3 focus on our personal thoughts. Those chapters introduce tools and practices for investigating our stories. Take a moment to think of something you have had rolling around in your head that distracted you or kept you up at night. Does that thought make you worry or feel stressed? Unexplored, such thoughts influence what and how we think and feel and how we interact. Conversely, becoming conscious of internal stories liberates us from their grip and taps into our inherent wisdom.

A word on *wisdom*. I like the Merriam-Webster Dictionary definition.

1a: ability to discern inner qualities and relationships:: INSIGHT

b: good sense: JUDGMENT

c: generally accepted belief // challenges what has become accepted wisdom among many historians—Robert Darnton

d: accumulated philosophical or scientific learning: KNOWLEDGE

2: a wise attitude, belief, or course of action:

3: the teachings of the ancient wise men:

Wisdom relies on our ability to reason productively about problems or breakdowns. Wise attributes include our intuition and insight, our ability to engage others with curiosity, decision-making based on conceptual and factual information, and humility to know the limits of our knowledge. By starting with our storytelling selves, we can accumulate a wiser perspective for reconsidering all conversations.

Chapter 1 explains how our brains, egos, awareness, and autopilot patterns serve or thwart our conversations.

Chapter 2 explores the crucial elements of our stories—facts, emotions, and opinions.

Chapter 3 introduces us to the consequential gap between our public words and our private thoughts—increasing our awareness of how it impacts our conversations.

Chapter 4 introduces four archetypal questions—desires, concerns, power dynamics, and standards of judgment—as a guide for investigating stories.

Let's begin breaking down our stories. You might laugh or cry as you engage with the committee, but in the end it will be worth the effort because you will be a better conversationalist.

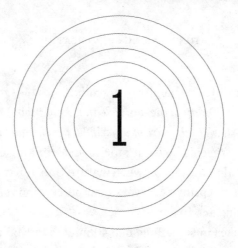

THE BIRTH OF STORIES

Reality is always kinder than the stories we tell about it.

—BYRON KATIE

We humans have been telling stories for millennia. These stories determine how we relate, parent, work, and love; what we value; and with whom we choose to wage war. They describe who we are (father/son, leader/follower, citizen/immigrant, conservative/liberal). They forge relationships (partnerships, marriages, friendships, colleagues). We entertain and educate one another through them (books, schools, universities, movies, fiction). And they activate our work together (contracts, employment, friends helping friends).

When life is chugging along, our story-making brains work beautifully, and we rarely notice the work that they do. Everything feels right, like home. Right now I'm sipping espresso, listening to music, talking to myself while editing my manuscript, and feeling the kick of caffeine. All the while, stories are weaving in and out of my mind effortlessly. Our stories exist on a broad spectrum, from the harmful (*I will never pass this trigonometry test*) to the helpful (*I'm ready to ace that master's degree*), from the prosaic (*Today is the day I clean up my inbox*) to the profound (*If I keep the faith and take care of myself, I'll get through this diagnosis*).

This chapter reveals how our stories and thinking emerge from an unconscious collaboration between nature and nurture. We explore how the brain is the primary driver of our perceptions and egos and our autopilot thinking and reacting.

The brain takes in something like 40 million bits of data per second. The average human brain contains 100 billion neurons, which form an incomprehensibly complex network with a ton of storage capacity, swirling with constant activity. Our brains manage a barrage of visual, auditory, tactile, and olfactory signals with blinding speed. And like magic, they filter the incoming data, connect dots, produce perceptions, make predictions, and help us make sense of the world. Our brains are also story-making machines, relentlessly monitoring what's happening in the moment, correlating it with our lives' experiences, and predicting what might happen next. They birth our stories. As story-making machines, they work around the clock, effortlessly, which is fundamental to our survival.

Neuroscience, an exciting frontier in brain research, is just beginning to map these complex cerebral circuitries. I can't do the research justice, but understanding the neuroscientific basics will help us understand conscious conversations. Our brains consist of the neocortex, entorhinal cortex, hippocampus, amygdala, left hemisphere, right hemisphere, the corpus callosum, and more. This incredible network supports biological switches, neurons, synapses, axons, and dendrites, which generate an intricate dance of electrical sparks that become our felt experience. A lot is going on under the hood, without conscious effort.

When the brain is doing its job, the person we become emerges from the collaboration between nature and nurture. Our DNA and all our inborn physical qualities constitute our nature. The whole of our life experiences plays a role in defining who we are, what we think, and how we feel and act (and react). Our native country, parents, education, society, and culture all constitute the nurtured self. From birth, we learn to survive by adopting concepts and developing patterns of thinking and emotions from our cultural milieu. Our DNA and social norms are inseparable, and this combination is at the root of our thinking, prejudices, judgments, emotions, and stories.

Depending on how the network is lighting up, we can experience memories of our first love, jealousy over a friend's success, anger at our overpowering boss, or pleasure from a piece of chocolate. Scientists, psychologists, and neuroscientists are still discovering the mysteries of this remarkable collaboration. Neuroscience is still in its infancy, but it's clear that there is much it can teach us about what makes us tick and why we do what we do.

Figure 1 is a broad view and simplification of the complexity of our minds and patterns. It's a picture to help us appreciate the origin and nature of our stories. External stimuli permeate our senses (vision, audition, olfaction, taste, and touch). Then the brain's complex systems—synthesizing nature and nurture—interpret and filter the incoming signals, make predictions, and form our perceptions. We then feel,

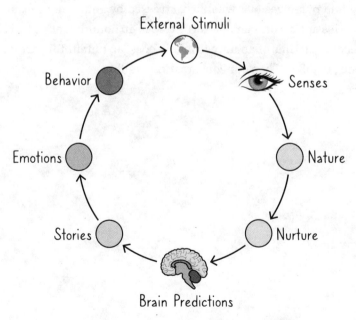

FIGURE 1: Our brain and stories

think, and act on our background assumptions, prejudices, and filtered perceptions. The process is circular. Our brain, body, and mind are inextricably linked, and they create narratives from the sounds, sights, temperatures, smells, tastes, and experiences we encounter. How we show up at any given moment is based on all we have felt, thought, and done before. All conscious and unconscious predictions and explanations are filtered through our past and woven into the present moment. Stated simply, we're explanation-oiled, judgment-filled, assumption-making machines.

This all works beautifully, but when a situation presents any significant deviation from our daily routine or when someone rubs up against an embedded story, our tried-and-true patterns of thought and behavior are interrupted, and we often react on autopilot. The stress of a flat tire, a demanding boss, a child in distress, a loss of money, or an unexpected medical diagnosis can cause us to react with fear, tears, anger, resentment, or disbelief. These are reasonable and normal reactions, but when we unconsciously get lost in the drama of the moment, we can easily find ourselves overwhelmed, stressed by emotion. Unexamined, our stories and reactionary patterns trap us in nonproductive loops, and we become victims of an unreasonable boss, an unfaithful partner, or a ranting neighbor. Then our conversations suffer.

Awareness

The ultimate value of life depends upon
awareness and the power of contemplation
rather than upon mere survival.

—ARISTOTLE

Without our miraculous unconscious brain activity, we would drown in data overload. While we go about our day-to-day activities, our mind manages our physical, psychological, emotional, and spiritual wellbeing. We generally operate as a bundle of habits and well-worn neural networks we didn't even choose.

Neuroscience confirms our capacity to operate at different levels of awareness. Awareness is the antidote to our conditioned habits. By cultivating awareness, we become mindful of our mind, including thoughts, feelings, and bodily sensations. We can think about our thinking, which is often called our *witnessing self.*

For a moment, close your eyes and simply pay attention to the thoughts and feelings arriving in your mind. No need to do anything other than observe. Notice what's arising—your breathing, your thoughts, your feelings, external sounds, and your bodily sensations. This simple exercise can give us a taste of mindfulness. We're conditioned to distraction, but when we pay attention, we discover that we often think without awareness that we are thinking. Whether through meditation or other methods (see Chapter 3, "Opinions and Private Conversations"), we can be conscious observers of our minds.

I have been meditating since I was eighteen years old. Through meditation, I learned to be a neutral observer of my thoughts, body, and feelings. Over time, my practice helped me become aware of the habits of my mind. Thoughts, sensations, and sounds came and went with no effort on my part. When I observe worrisome or negative thoughts or judgments, a space is created between me (the observer) and the thoughts. Over time, the distractions of the mind's comings and goings produce a detachment from them, and we can experience a separate conscious self. I have always liked the metaphor of consciousness as the clear blue sky and our streaming thoughts as clouds coming and going. Like the blue sky, our consciousness is always present. But as the skies cloud over, so too are our awareness and consciousness clouded over by our thoughts. Meditation is a practice that allows us to experience an always present clear consciousness.

If you're interested in trying meditation, there's a simple practice at the end of this chapter. No beliefs, special equipment, or gurus are required. It's just you, your mind, and a little time. Apps like Sam Harris's Waking Up, Dan Harris's Ten Percent Happier, and Calm are also useful.

Any work we do to increase awareness of our internal patterns directly affects our interactions with others. With my increased understanding of conversations, I have become more aware of myself in conversation and more perceptive of others. But I'm far from perfect, and there are days when my worries and reactions get the best of me (I have a particular aversion to service incompetence, to name one).

Changing unproductive patterns takes time. If I snap at a person helping me with a technical or financial problem, I might not become aware of my failing until hours later. The key to changing that pattern is noticing and noting its harmful effects. Instead of brushing off the frustration or blaming others, if we recognize their harm, we can investigate the pattern (more on this process in Chapter 3) and practice undoing it. With attention and some luck, on my next call with a service person, I might notice my trigger within two minutes or even two seconds and wake up in time to change the negativity of the conversation into one of mutual respect. Then I'm far likelier to get the service I need.

With increased awareness, our habitual background thoughts and judgments become less domineering, and we can catch ourselves in time to shift our reaction and a conversation. Minimizing judgment of our patterns helps us find humor in them so we can enjoy a good laugh. Humor is a great stress reliever and can lighten up most conversations.

I grew up with a racist step-grandfather. His unexamined assumptions, judgments, and prejudices seeped into my unconscious. My brain took in his stories about people of color hook, line, and sinker. As a child, I didn't consciously choose to adopt his judgments, but in the context of my family, my grandfather's words had authority, and his beliefs infused into mine. When I became aware of these harmful, racist stories, I was surprised at how ingrained they were. It took time and conscious effort to recognize and acknowledge this pattern and change my thinking, but I can still hear distant whispers of his words in my mind. I know that they aren't true, and I'm thankful that I'm free of them.

It takes courage to inquire into our thoughts and beliefs. My inquiries were an eye-opener. Questions arose: Why did I feel insecure around certain people? Why did my mouth go dry when I was challenged? Why did I cry at one event and feel untouched by another? Why was I thinking one thing and saying something else? Is it possible that what I believed was simply one way of seeing, looking, and feeling?

Increasing our awareness of our thoughts while we are engaged in conversation with ourselves and others is an important first step toward having conscious conversations.

Autopilot

Unconscious processes of the brain hide useless information from us while bringing data vital for survival to the surface. The autopilot brain is a significant determinant of how we experience and navigate the world. Many of our stories run on autopilot. They quickly move us into action to avoid an oncoming tiger or truck. And they save us energy so we don't need to stop and ask, *How should I make my morning coffee? What's the best route to the office? How do I save a file?* But they also have drawbacks.

Our brains work so quickly that we simply don't question our background stories. When we're mindless, we engage in conversations loaded with private thoughts, judgments, emotions, and egos—*I'm so done with this idiot! Why on earth can't people be on time? How is it that people can believe that political B.S.?*

As I write these words, the United States is in unprecedented political turmoil. This political climate is a perfect example of how difficult it is to be mindful and wake up out of autopilot. Facts are in doubt, the press is polarized, and constructive conversations are rare. The general public and politicians are all crying foul. My clients and friends on both sides of the aisle email and text me in disbelief. "How can they want to teach that in our schools?" "How on earth can they believe those idiots in Congress?" "The Supreme Court is nothing but another political arm. Maybe it's time to expand the bench."

Like it or not, as life unfolds, it often isn't aligned with our story of what should be happening. The difference between what we want to happen and the reality of what's happening is a source of suffering. When we don't like what we see, the battle between our stories and reality—small (the weather) and large (relationships)—plays out in our minds, feelings, and conversations. "Bosses shouldn't act that way." "Men shouldn't treat women that way." "She shouldn't spend so much on shoes." "Governments can't manage anything."

○ ○

A talented client, Paul, was desperate to become a director in his company. He had a good story going in his head: *The next director position belongs to me.* In his mind, his colleagues were incompetent, but he had worked hard and earned the position. His ego was whispering that this imminent next step up the corporate ladder was his ticket to more money and greater prestige—a gratifying story. He wanted and needed that job.

Here's the rub: Paul's unchecked story had him stressed out. Anxious, impatient, and obsessed, he began to second-guess himself: *Should I speak up? Are they listening to my opinions? What do I need to do to get them to recognize how good I am?* He questioned what he said, how he dressed, and what others thought of him. His anxious behavior led to an outcome opposite of his goal. Rather than being present and confidently speaking his opinions and sharing his ideas, he showed up as insecure and nervous.

When the announcement came that he wasn't promoted to director, he was crushed. Reality didn't match his story about what should have happened. He told himself that the company's decision was wrongheaded, unjust, and unhinged. He suffered because his blinding story kept him from understanding why others weren't perceiving him as the perfect candidate. He was depressed for weeks.

Coincidentally, we were introduced to one another and started to work together. First, I asked Paul to do some journaling. He wrote down his story with his judgments and assumptions unedited. His words on paper revealed a big gap between his need to land that job and the reality on the ground. While doing this work, he came to see the negative impact of his neediness and insecurities. Armed with new observations, he recognized that his unchecked story was his own worst enemy.

Paul's anxiety lessened as he adopted new practices and reframed his story. He slowly gained more confidence and found his voice in meetings. He closed the gap between his blind desires and the reality of his situation. Paul had new insights and began to try on new ways of showing up. Over time, he got his promotion, and he was a better leader for the work that he did on himself.

o o

We function well with our background stories running on autopilot—until we don't. We can cruise along like Paul, stressed out and sticking with our stories of what *should* be happening. We can do that for minutes, days, years, or decades—until we run smack-dab into a person or an event that slams us back into reality.

When we pay attention to our habitual reactionary patterns, we will inevitably encounter our ego.

The Ego

*It seems to me that most of us are not aware, not only of
what we are talking about but of our environment, the
colors around us, the people, the shape of the trees, the
clouds, the movement of water. Perhaps it is because we
are so concerned with ourselves, with our own petty little
problems, our own ideas, our own pleasures, pursuits and
ambitions that we are not objectively aware.*

—J. KRISHNAMURTI, thinker and spiritual teacher

As we observe ourselves in conversation, we come face to face with the
ego. *Don't be such an idiot. They're so wrong. Who are they to talk down
to me?* One job of our ego is to identify with every element (i.e., judgments, prejudices, and beliefs) of our stories and to defend them at all
costs, even in the face of inconvenient facts. When you listen to your
mind's background commentary, you will hear your ego yapping away.
While you're frowning and agreeing with one neighbor about another
barking dog, your ego is whispering, *I can't believe this guy is such a
jackass!*

The ego would be pleased if we never questioned our stories and
peeked at the mind's underbelly. It prefers that we stay on autopilot and
not rock the boat. So when you ask questions like, *Why am I reacting this
way?*—the answer in your head might sound like this: *Because I'm right
and they're wrong!* Or maybe this: *Why am I feeling so insecure? Because
I'm an idiot, I'd better keep my mouth shut.* These answers are the ego's
way of clinging to a story while suppressing our curiosity and awareness. The ego wastes no time in its defense. It's tricky, quick, addictive,
and convincing.

The shape-shifting ego can be our victor, victim, critic, or denier.
It will assume any form necessary to defend its assumptions and sub-
sequent narratives. As we begin to witness and increase awareness of
our stories, the ego will reveal itself in all its defensive glory. It's adept

at assuring us that our stories should remain intact and unquestioned. As I began to observe and question the prejudices and judgments in my stories, I slowly realized that my ego was always ready with an explanation: *Of course, they're wrong. How can they be so stupid?* Or, *Don't be so hesitant. Get out there and defend yourself.* My arrogant and belittling ego was a deafening critic.

With the ego running the show, we can, at any moment, see ourselves as brilliant or idiotic. At a party, we might glance around the room and find ourselves thinking, *These people are dimwitted.* On the other hand, we could be driving to a family get-together, stomach tightening, thinking, *I'm such a failure. How am I going to face them? I was drunk when I visited last.* Negative judgment of others and self-judgment is the ego's specialty.

The ego identifies with our stories and ensures that our environs, actions, and reactions are all about *me, me,* and *me.* It's always sure that it knows how events should unfold and what we should do. Paramount to the ego is our belief that our story is the "truth." It leaves little room for doubt, questions, or curiosity. When the ego is in charge, we have to be right.

Investigating our stories starts a process of disengaging from the ego. A crucial part of awareness is paying attention to our autopilot egoic thinking with nonjudgmental curiosity. Judging our judge only sends us on an endless loop of negativity. By acknowledging the ego with empathic curiosity, we can begin to tame it.

○ ○

I have a thing about being on time. I wasn't aware of this habit until my second marriage to a lovely woman who has a different relationship with time. I can be ready to go and get out of the house a lot faster than my wife can. Years ago, as I was sitting in the car, ready to go, I found myself impatiently stewing. *What on earth could be taking her so long?* I got all twisted up, and I built up a good head of steam to unload on her ... or on the gas pedal. It seemed pretty clear-cut to me. I was right because I was always on time, and she was wrong because she was always late.

After filling the car with my unspoken, angry judgments, we drove to our destination in stressed silence.

I was in lockdown and blinded by my ego's attachment to the "right way," which carried my beliefs about time, preparation, and lateness. I was clueless about how much more time she needed to get ready than I did. I showered, towel-dried my hair, threw on some jeans and a semi-clean shirt, slipped on my shoes, grabbed my keys, and headed for the door. What could be simpler? My ego was full of righteous indignation. When that happened, we both stressed out, which made for a pretty crappy start to a night out.

This relationship aha happened while I was studying the ontology of language with the Newfield Group. Here was a chance to put theoretical ideas into practice. I practiced catching my emotions and the accompanying self-righteous story and ego in action. Curiously observing my auto-emotional reactions helped me unhook from them, and I was able to take a good hard look at my uninvestigated judgments.

Believe it or not, it took this breakdown for me to become aware of my wife's needs, timing, and patterns. I came to accept how much she relishes her shower and bathroom spa time, enjoying the time to care for her body, her hair, her face, her clothing, and her jewelry. Her comfortable patterns and way of preparing for a night out could not be more different from mine.

I discovered that my story wasn't the truth by working with this mundane, everyday dilemma. It was loaded with a bucketful of judgments, prejudices, and assumptions. When I was able to witness and catch my triggers in real time, I could stop stewing and arguing.

As I woke up from autopilot reactions, we were able to talk about our patterns. We learned to appreciate our differences and talked about them without the stress. We agreed on some ways to change our rituals and test them out. We both shared a desire to be on time to events. I took responsibility for my impatience, and she agreed that she could be more aware of her routine and the time she needed to get out the door.

It seems obvious now, but it took a little planning and conscious effort to alter our pattern. My wife needed to stop whatever she was doing one hour before we needed to leave, and I could play a game of solitaire on my phone, practice the piano, or even ask if there was a way to help her rather than stewing. Our new agreement was critical for changing the dance. Eventually, we were more relaxed when getting ready to go out. In this simple but powerful experience, I checked my ego, and through our conversations, we eliminated a bunch of frustrations.

o o

Our everyday interactions at work and home provide us with plenty of material to work with. In the remaining chapters, we'll dissect the heart of our sense-making stories and experiment with new tools for working with them.

PRACTICES

○ Begin to note your triggers (e.g., the kids, your boss, your in-laws, loud music, a neighbor's dog, traffic). Is there a pattern of impatience, frustration, insecurities?

○ Rather than berating your ego, try befriending it by simply observing its message. This is a powerful way to witness rather than to blindly accept the thoughts.

○ Practice being mindful at home and at work and observe what's happening in the moment to see what thought patterns seem to repeat themselves. How do you feel different when you take a moment to be mindful?

○ Simply note your recurring automatic reactions and emotions on any given day. Be mindful of your judgments and the emotions that accompany them.

○ How do you feel differently when you're simply observing yourself or others with curiosity rather than with judgment?

Here's a meditation practice based on Vipassana, a well-regarded, well-researched method:

1. Find a comfortable sitting position, your spine straight.

2. Take a few breaths to settle into your seat.

3. Close your eyes and continue taking a few breaths. Notice your body sitting in the chair. Notice any bodily sensations that arise—warmth, tense muscles, a grumbling tummy.

4. Gradually bring your attention to your breath. Pick the spot where you most feel your breath—your nose, tummy, chest.

5. Allow your attention to rest there, noticing your breath coming in and out, naturally.

6. As you pay attention to your breath, you will simultaneously begin to notice thoughts, emotions, and bodily sensations. Observe them as they arise.

7. When you notice you have been distracted by thoughts, sounds, or feelings (this is your mind running its pattern, which is totally normal), gently return your attention to your breath.

8. Continue keeping your breath at the center of your attention, noting all thoughts, sounds, and sensation as objects of consciousness, arising and passing through.

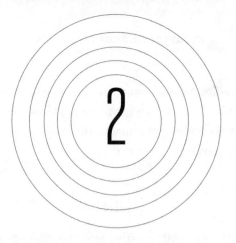

EMOTIONS, FACTS, AND STORIES

If your emotional abilities aren't in hand,
if you don't have self-awareness, if you are not able to
manage your distressing emotions, if you can't have
empathy and have effective relationships, then no matter
how smart you are, you are not going to get very far.

—DANIEL GOLEMAN, author of *Emotional Intelligence*

Being aware of our stories is a good start, but to understand the considerable role they play in conversation, we need to investigate their components.

Stories break down into three fundamental elements: emotions, facts, and opinions. As demonstrated in Figure 1 in the previous chapter, first incoming signals get interpreted and filtered, then we perceive what's happening. Whatever the event, our emotions reflect our experience with the truths we hold, the facts available to us, and our opinions. Our senses, beliefs, and social constructs can deceive us, allowing us only to see, hear, and feel what aligns with our stories. When we're on autopilot, our stories keep humming along. Our emotions, facts, and opinions are jumbled together, and they become fuzzy in our minds. By taking a deeper dive into each element, we can tease them apart and gain insight into how each element impacts our thinking, behavior, and conversations. Let's start with emotions.

Emotions

Thoughts and stories—both positive and negative—generate our emotional reactions. Our stories are a significant factor in determining if we're happy or sad, relaxed or anxious, clear-minded or confused. When life is positive, effortless, and beautiful, we're proud, loving, and satisfied. But when life doesn't match up with our stories and expectations, our emotions signal a disruption of our thinking and judgmental patterns. When we're off-kilter, it's easy to be consumed with displeasure, anger, or frustration, which leaves us stressed and feeling crappy. Whether we experience emotions as tears of hurt or tears of laughter, they aren't an end in themselves.

As Proust so beautifully put it, "Our emotions are geologic upheavals of thought." (See Figure 2.) They aren't innocent, primal reactions. Our beliefs about good and evil, right and wrong, and just and unjust surface as emotions. It turns out that our emotions don't drive our thinking; rather, our thinking drives our emotions. Unsettling emotions are a signal that it's time to examine the harm in our thoughts and stories.

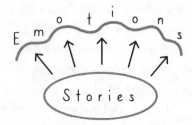

FIGURE 2: Emotions as reflections of our stories

The feeling of knowing what's is happening in our bodies is called *interoception,* for example, the experience of a racing heart, a grumbling belly, a chilled body, or tense muscles. Interoception is the internal process that helps us experience those things and is often called our sixth sense. Our hard-working brain is doing its job, collecting data from our internal organs, skin, and eyes and sending chemical signals through our bodies. It's why we can ask, *How do I feel?* Only we can bear witness to how we feel. When we're out of sorts, our bodily sensations are the first sign of upset, and they are a signal that we should pay heed. Don't ignore them or brush them aside. And our feelings, emotions, and underlying thoughts get expressed consciously and unconsciously through our eyes, skin, tone of voice, and body language. A tight chest, a red face, or teary eyes are signals that we should investigate our stories.

In conversation, awareness of our interoceptive senses and emotional reactivity is essential to our ability to self-regulate, maintain our mental health, and connect socially. Interoceptive and emotional awareness have significant impacts on our conversations.

The meditation exercise in Chapter 1 is a complementary practice for learning to observe our thinking and stories.

Here's a quote from Lisa Feldman Barrett's book *How Emotions Are Made*:

> In short, we find that your emotions are not built-in but made from more basic parts. They are not universal but vary from culture to culture. They are not triggered, you create them. They emerge as a combination of the physical properties of your body, a flexible brain that wires itself to whatever environment it develops in, and your culture and upbringing, which provide that environment. Emotions are real, but not in the objective sense that molecules or neurons are real. They are real in the same sense that money is real—that is, hardly an illusion, but a product of human agreement.

Our emotional palette runs the full spectrum, from fear to love. We're all wired differently. Some of us have minds that are supersensitive to the outside world, and we react accordingly. Others are less sensitive and reactive to external stimuli. Awareness of our level of sensitivity can help us understand our reactions and navigate our interactions.

Have you ever been to a science exhibit that included a funnel-shaped slide? When you roll a coin on its edge down the funnel, it picks up speed until it spins so quickly that it becomes a shiny, unrecognizable blur at the bottom. That's an apt metaphor for the broad spectrum of our emotional experiences. For many events and interactions, we can remain calm on the upside of the funnel, feeling positive, open, and tolerant. But fears ranging from a concern about the weather ruining our day to a horrifying fear of losing our job can start a downward spiral, inducing frustration, stress, and anger. As we spiral down, our thinking gets blurry, and we're unable to observe, think, or react with clarity. At the bottom everything seems negative and problematic. Being at the bottom of the spiral is a sure sign that we should check in with our body's interoceptive signals and investigate thoughts and fears that could be the root of our negative emotions.

Not all fears are bad. Many deep-seated patterns are built-in interoceptive reactions necessary for survival. The fears that spurred our ancestors to run so as not to be eaten by something with large teeth are lifesaving. More often than not, our survival instincts keep us out of trouble. We jump from the path of the oncoming truck. We heed warning signs that point to the possibility of losing our job or our home. If our power goes out because we forgot to pay the bill, we immediately drive to the appropriate office with our payment. But the parts of our brains that protect us from real danger can also project imagined threats, causing our overactive minds to worry and overreact.

I map the funnel this way: At the top of the spiral is love, an expanded state of understanding, compassion, and peace. At the bottom is fear, a state of stress and negativity (see Figure 3). The varied emotions we experience daily fall somewhere between those two extremes. I think about the opposite ends of the spiral as light/open vs. heavy/contracted. Within the spectrum of love and fear, many antithetical emotions track at the top and bottom of the spiral (e.g., compassion vs. condemnation, humility vs. arrogance, curiosity vs. defensiveness).

Love

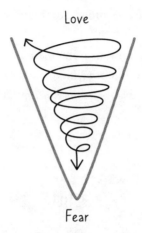

Fear

FIGURE 3: Spiral of emotions

This simple diagram can remind us to take note of where we are on the funnel when our feelings and bodies are calling for attention.

When we catch ourselves spinning downward, we can wake up in the moment, become aware of our reactive patterns, and note where we are on the spiral. *Am I spinning down and angry? What he said has me spiraling down with worry.* With practice, we become better observers, and we can gradually change an unproductive pattern over time. Our physical responses, such as contracting muscles and rampant stress hormones, will decrease, and our tendency to startle or snap will diminish. My story about my impatience with my wife is an example of me catching myself spiraling. Triggered by our pattern, I was taking lots of trips down the funnel, driven by my fear of being late. I was impatient with my wife and became angry and stressed. When I took the time to reflect on my emotional reactions, I recognized my tense body, investigated my finger-pointing judgments, and realized that I needed to rethink my patterns.

Noticing our emotions while we're on the spiral dramatically impacts how we interact with others, allowing us to better manage and change our emotions and thoughts, which subsequently allows us to inch our way up the funnel. Once we thought, *She's impossible,* or *With this idiot in charge, we'll never make the deadline.* But now we're more attuned and sensitive, and we can be less judgmental and more empathetic toward others.

Our emotional reactions are an open invitation to examine the reality of any moment. *What am I imagining or making up? What am I feeling right now? What assumptions am I making? What are the facts? What's true?*

Next, we will look at facts and stories.

PRACTICES

○ Practice catching yourself spinning up or down the spiral.

○ Investigate what fear (minor to major) might be lurking in the background of your reactions.

○ Note what feelings and emotions accompany your stories. Are some emotions more prevalent for you?

○ What feelings and emotions do you experience when sliding down the spiral versus moving up?

Indisputable Facts

Get your facts first, then you can
distort them as you please.

—MARK TWAIN

In order to continue deconstructing and investigating our stories, we must turn our attention to facts. In the world of stories, facts are a welcome, stable element—solid ground to stand on. In a sane world, they are inarguable. But our stories often deceive us because facts can surface uncomfortable truths that we won't or can't accept.

To see proof of that unwillingness to respect facts, you need look no further than the political arena where facts have been under constant attack over the last few years. There's no such thing as "alternative facts." We have seen far too many people cherry-picking a few convenient facts to validate the story they are hooked on while disregarding facts that don't support their position. Facts are crucial to civil society and democracy, but because of the power of language and stories, we're susceptible to their abuse and the instability they generate.

Facts are born from our shared human capacities. For the most part, we humans perceive the objective world in the same way (minus a few outliers like those who are color blind or who have sensory impairments). We have the sight of a human, not an eagle. We have the olfactory nerves of a human, not a dog. We hear in the range of 64–23,000 hertz, whereas porpoises hear in the range of 75–150,000 hertz. Our limited but shared range of senses allows us to agree on what's loud vs. quiet, black vs. white, solid vs. liquid, up vs. down, and stinky vs. fragrant.

Through shared social constructs, we measure, document, categorize, and declare things as factual, and we bestow upon them the label *objective truth*. Yet even these shared truths are mutable. The truth we hold at any time can be trumped by new facts. Discoveries in science and engineering can reveal new facts. The myth that held that Earth was the flat center of the universe survived for many centuries in many cultures.

Nicolaus Copernicus's heliocentric cosmology model began to dispel the myth. Galileo Galilei's cosmological observations proved that Earth and the other planets revolved around the sun. Likewise, what were thought to be untreatable illnesses centuries ago are now, thanks to modern medicine, treatable. In the late eighteenth century, Abigail Adams was an early adopter of the first primitive smallpox vaccine, which saved her children's lives.

On the surface, facts and truth may seem simple-minded and obvious, but they are regularly weaponized and debated. Our ability to have conscious conversations relies on the inarguable, common-sense meaning of facts, which are based on documentable experience and observations. While our understanding of the truth might vary depending on our religion or spirituality, our shared reality is a crucial element of meaningful conversations. The firm ground that facts provide is the perfect antidote to futile debates with people who claim that "my truth" and "your truth" exist in separate realities. Without facts, our feelings, stories, and opinions would send us adrift, and we would have little common reality, making it difficult to know right from wrong or good from evil.

In spite of our varied histories, experiences, and perceptions of the world, for conversation's sake, what is is. The reality of a flat tire, an abusive boss, inequality, racism, misogyny, and climate change can only be argued if we ignore facts and declare our opinions and stories as the truth.

Facts come to the rescue when our stories conflict with reality. Our story tells us that we deserve that job, then—wham!—we get laid off. We think we will have fun at the party, but then we arrive in a crappy mood because of the fight we had with our partner. We expect our teenage kids to do the right thing, but then our child calls in the middle of the night to tell us that they were just arrested for a DUI.

Sometimes life unfolds in ways that we don't want or expect. When we can't or don't accept life as it has been served up, we spin out, which sets us up for a battle with reality. I know of no one who has won a fight with reality.

We find ourselves in disbelief, unable to see clearly, looking at the world from the narrow perspective of our stories. And when we ask ourselves,

How could they be so stupid? or *Why is this happening?* We're in a nonacceptance state of mind, a mood of resentment (see Figure 4). *Life shouldn't be this way.* My upset with my wife's delay created misery that lasted for hours. As my anger set in and tension built in my body, I unconsciously slid into resentment. We couldn't talk, so we sulked in our crankiness.

When we can catch ourselves spiraling from anywhere on the funnel downward toward stress, we can take a breath, slow down, and check out the facts. In my case, I was stuck and stressed from a maddening story about being late. I uncovered a few facts: I was angry and she wasn't, my ideas about being late were very different from hers, and the ten minutes it took me to get ready was far from sufficient for my wife. Another piece of evidence was the fact that my upset consistently created unnecessary tension for us.

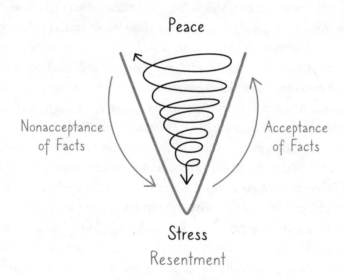

FIGURE 4: The spiral of peace vs. resentment

When we find the courage to accept facts that are upsetting, it doesn't mean we like or approve of them. I can continue to dislike being late, but when my wife and I talked about and accepted the facts of our differences, we found our way to a win-win solution. But, on hot issues like gun control, refugees, birth control, education, and taxes, it is extremely unsettling and discouraging when the facts don't fit our story. Our attachment to our stories and strong opinions makes it difficult to shift from nonacceptance to accepting the facts. Life is far more peaceful when we can accept facts as they are.

Our behaviors in conversation are also facts. Our words, reactions, body language, and voices are factual, a done deal. We have all had to face the facts when we say one thing and do another, act out our aggressions, lose our temper and scream at the kids, or lie about our actions. What we do is recordable, memorable, and confirmable.

The stories from voices with authority, leaders, parents, priests, and teachers have a significant impact on how we think and what we believe. We innocently adopt their espoused opinions as facts.

Growing up, when I got sick helping my grandfather skin a deer in the basement, my father would say, "Stop getting sick and man up!" My grandfather would admonish me, saying, "You're not a big enough man!" My younger brother wasn't born until I was nine years old, so I grew up with three older sisters. Like many households in that era, my sisters could show their emotions, but I was supposed to "man up." I had to stuff it all. In the 1950s, men were taught to hide their emotions. "Boys don't cry." "Hide your feelings." "Be a man."—those were the mantras we boys were taught from birth. After years of painful lessons, I woke up to just how traumatic this social construct was. Sadly, these same patterns persist in many parts of the world, and they're the root of much masculine-macho misconduct.

At a deep level, this never sat well with me. I had all sorts of pent-up feelings, and I often went to my room alone with my upset. It wasn't fair. While unaware, I had no power to create the rules. But the pronouncements of male authority figures carry a lot of weight for young men. For many years, I unconsciously adopted the story that I wasn't man enough. It had long-lasting consequences for my relationships, professional life, and self-esteem.

That story had me in its spell, and I spun down the spiral of self-doubt. Eventually, through my studies, I investigated this story starting with the facts. I was 6'0" and 180 pounds. I had been a successful professional musician and was on my second career as an architect. I had a wife and two amazing sons who I loved and supported. I had good, loving friends and siblings. The list of blessings and accomplishments went on and on. After unearthing these facts, my story began to unravel. Slowly but surely, I realized that the story that I wasn't big enough wasn't my *truth*. By accepting the facts, I busted a toxic story.

We all have stories about making avoidable mistakes, stressing over serious misunderstandings, or living with limiting beliefs based on assumptions and premature conclusions not rooted in fact. We have experienced influential leaders ignoring the facts, charging ahead blindly. Or dysfunctional families ending up in litigation over finances. Or nations launching wars because their egotistic narcissistic leaders disavowed facts.

Depending on how facts contradict our worldview, acknowledging and accepting them can be onerous. It takes courage to explore inconvenient truths when we uncover them. Our triggered reactions might send us spinning, but reflecting on the facts won't deceive us, and we can slowly move ourselves up the funnel. Surfacing and accepting facts prepares us to explore the next element of our stories: our cherished opinions.

PRACTICES

○ What events on any given day send you spiraling down? What are your body's interoceptive signals—a tight belly or shoulders, a red face, a dry mouth?

○ What bare-bone facts of a situation can't be questioned? Are the facts misaligned with your expectations?

○ What are you afraid of? Are there facts that could counter your fears? Are you missing any facts about this situation?

○ In a confrontational situation/conversation, can you unearth facts that both parties agree on?

○ Take note: When you acknowledge and accept the facts, how do you feel differently?

OPINIONS AND
PRIVATE CONVERSATIONS

*A great many people think they are thinking when they are
merely rearranging their prejudices.*

—WILLIAM JAMES,
American philosopher and psychologist

After working with our emotions and facing the facts, we open the
Pandora's opinions box. True to the myth, the world of opinions
is full of blessings and trouble—blessings because our beliefs and
judgments help us assess and navigate life, trouble because we unconsciously identify with those views and conclusions. Curse or blessing,
our emotions, words, and actions reflect our opinions. Storytelling conversations thrive on our opinions. How boring would life be if each of us
interpreted and gave meaning to facts in exactly the same way?

We would be confused and rudderless without our interpretations
and individual quirks. In conversation, opinions play a prominent role

overriding facts, and it is far too common in dialogue for the two to be inflated. A firm foundation of facts can support opinions, but our subjective opinions should not be confused with facts. A leader's desire and requirement for a product design—i.e., a more powerful battery—is likely to be misaligned with what their engineer can design based on physics. A board member's opinion for a six-month financial strategy will likely differ from what the CFO's forecast is projecting. Or, my friend's strong feelings about keeping a relationship alive could blind him to the reality of a partner gone astray.

Our opinions are deeply embedded so we will take them apart to find the blessings and avoid their curse. The first honest look we take will most likely be uncomfortable and surprising. We will uncover strong, dominant, unspoken thoughts such as these: *How on earth can he be so stubborn? His decisions are never going to get this project on track! She's crazy for blocking me from all social media.*

From birth, we effortlessly absorb what's right and wrong, good and bad, possible and impossible, and scary and peaceful from our parents, teachers, friends, and culture. Our identities rely on our opinions, so much so that it is easy to forget what they are: a collection of assumptions, concerns, judgments, and standards. While comforting, left unchecked, they are the root cause of most misunderstandings and miscommunications.

Predictably, our ego, skilled at defending our positions, loves to join in. For emotionally charged issues, we can quickly feel indignation when challenged. *I am right, and they just don't get it.* A *confirmation bias* is a defense of our position, seeking and interpreting information to support our beliefs, or misrepresenting data to justify our position. Blinded by our prejudices, we seek out friends and colleagues whose views align with ours and rebuff people who oppose our opinions— which is comforting, but far from courageous. Our brains react by sending stress response signals that drive us deeper into judgment and negativity. Such thoughts are noisy and discombobulated, and if we leave them unchecked, they become troublesome, and we end up into loopy ruminations.

To avoid spinning out, we practice being a witness of them. As neutral observers, we have a fighting chance to detach from them and think about our thinking. We note our emotional reactions, become aware of the underlying thoughts, search for facts, move up the spiral, and do some sleuthing to take a shot at changing a reactive, unproductive pattern.

Private Conversations

Ourself behind ourself, concealed—
Should startle most.

—EMILY DICKINSON

This work with facts, emotions, and opinions brings us face to face with a phenomenon of the mind that humans have been struggling with since the dawn of humanity: our unspoken private conversations, what I called the committee earlier. Private conversations are what we're thinking and feeling when sitting through a meeting, walking down the street, listening to music in the car, or telling our colleague that she is doing a good job. Ethan Kross, in his book *Chatter: The Voice in Our Head, Why It Matters, and How to Harness It,* lays out behavioral and brain research that explains how our inner self-talk can stress our relationships, affect our health, and tank conversations.

Our internal dialogues are industrious, fast moving, and disorienting. As unspoken participants of our stories, the committee has a few things to teach us and they are inextricably linked to our thinking that their words can serve us well and also be the source of much suffering. Our inner dialogues can help us work through a sticky problem, ramble on to get something off our chest, or positively motivate us and kick us into action.

However, inner diatribes also set us spinning down the funnel with fear, disbelief, pent-up anger, resentment, and plenty of blame and shame. For that reason, we ignore them, hold them at bay, or curse them, for the most part. As unconscious parts of our opinions, they can run amok and become dominant paralyzing voices. Triggered, stressed, or emotionally reactive, the committee loves to scrutinize, judge, accuse, and avoid conflict, specializing in regrets of the past and worries about the future. In conversations with our boss, colleagues, or kids, we think we're maintaining our cool while our private conversations are busy producing negative, unchecked stories.

Recently, a client named Christina started an exciting new role as a project coordinator on a major new initiative. As she began her new work, the owner of the initiative, Raheem, Christina's leader, decided that she should partner with the HR group, reasoning that they should be a partner since, in the end, HR would own the rollout. This was not good news for Christina. A few years back, she had an unpleasant encounter (long story) with her then leader, Agnes, the VP of HR. Christina immediately knew in her gut that Agnes's old stories about her would find their way to Raheem. I spoke with her a few days after the initial meeting to kick off the project. She was in tears and spinning down with fear that Agnes could hijack her work and her career for the foreseeable future. While she was trying her best to be professional in the meeting, her internal dialogue was running wild. *Why can't she let the past go? I can't believe this bitch won't give me a chance. I am doomed. She is going to screw up this great opportunity. Okay, just shut up and keep your thoughts and ideas to yourself. I just want her out of my life.* After that meeting, Christina began to second guess herself. *Should I speak up? What if she tells Raheem that I am hard to work with?*

Everything was negative. She was hijacked by her past worries and problems with Agnes. We started by looking for some events and facts to counter her emotional reactions. After Agnes was no longer her leader, Christina sought out coaching and worked on her leadership communication style, striving for collaboration with her colleagues and others. She was proud of the work she had done on her communication style and the success it had brought, and she had recently gotten some terrific feedback from a VP who she had helped out in a bind. The counter facts to her private conversation calmed her down considerably. We also talked through what she could do and not do in the current situation. Christina could practice catching her old triggers before they took hold in her head. Eventually, that gave her enough time to catch herself and stop the spinning. She could also refocus on kicking off the project and bring her best collaborative efforts to future meetings. She could not change Agnes, and she could not undo the past, but she could change her negative triggers. Recentered, she shared her concerns with Raheem about the old stories haunting her and assured him of her commitment to being a good leader. She requested feedback if he saw anything about her communications that confirmed old stories or that gave him concerns. An hour of surfacing, reflecting, and reconsidering her private conversation was what she needed to come to her senses and regain her confidence.

The investigation of our opinions reveals the gap between our internal private conversations (the committee) and our public conversations (what we say out loud). Our public conversations are facts, observable and documentable. If a boss asks, "How are you going to manage this new budget?" or your future father-in-law asks, "Exactly how do you intend to take care of my daughter?" a video recorder can capture the words, the tone of voice, and the body language. So the spoken words are factual events, even if they are full of assumptions and judgments. They can't be denied, no matter how they're received or interpreted—words spoken matter.

Simultaneously, our subconscious processing, automatic assumptions, inner thoughts, and accompanying feelings run in the background of our minds. When inner dialogues turn into a rogue diatribe, they're almost always toxic. Although they're unspoken, seemingly private, and often unconscious, they're rarely hidden. Like it or not, our inner dialogue hangs out in plain sight, on display through our tone of voice and our body language, available for all to see. Bodies don't lie.

Let's say that you're telling the boss, with as much confidence as you can muster, that the budget is in good shape. While you're speaking, you're thinking, *His decisions have gotten us into trouble, but I can't tell him now—he'll explode!* Or maybe you're chatting with your future father-in-law, and he asks you to protect his daughter from the vicissitudes of life, and you respond by saying, "Of course, I have every intention of taking care of your daughter." While saying those words, you might think, *This guy doesn't trust me! I wonder what his expectations are?*

In certain work situations, we might be thinking, *I want to get out of here, and I don't like you or your silly ideas,* but we might say, "Sure, I'd be happy to talk to you about the project." Or we might think, *You're so attractive, and I really want to get to know you better,* but we might avert our eyes and say, "Nice to see you, too." Private conversations short-circuit our interactions. They feed on themselves, generating fearful emotions and sending us spinning down the funnel. They can keep us from kissing our loved ones goodbye in the morning, distract us from our schedule, keep us from being present during crucial meetings, or wake us up with worries at 3 A.M.

Exploring our private and public conversations and closing the gap between them can be frightening, but it is ultimately freeing. The benefits are personal, relational, and productive. Rather than staying trapped in multiple layers of distress, we can wake up out of autopilot, catch our triggers, move up the funnel, change our thinking, and take responsibility for transforming a conversation.

Here's my theory: the bigger the gap between our negative private conversations and spoken public conversations, the more stress we will experience. Closing the gap between our private and public conversations is fundamental to shifting how we show up in conversations. As our private conversations happily run in the background, never seeing the light of day, they saddle us with unnecessary stress and dysfunction. As we become mindful of them, it seems we have only two options: bring them out of the dark by blurting them out loud or suppress them and keep them in the dark.

Sometimes we're tempted to stop being so damn polite and just say what we're thinking. *It would be more honest if I were to just let 'em have it.* A physical, feel-good rush of self-righteousness often accompanies this impulse—something along the lines of, *Oh man, letting loose is the way to go!* But if we're in a difficult conversation, our anxiety or anger is triggered, and we say our private thoughts out loud, we will most likely regret the emotional liberation hours later. Blurting out our negative inner thoughts, chock-full of emotions, is limiting and can have devastating consequences. In most instances, blurting out our private conversation damages relationships at work and at home, and it rarely helps us achieve our goals.

The other response to managing our internal thoughts is to bottle them up. We hold them in, consciously or unconsciously, and quietly soldier on. Bottled up, they build up and hurt us physically, causing muscular tension, headaches, high blood pressure, and other physical maladies. Toxic thoughts don't magically disintegrate, and over time, they can hit a boiling point and unexpectedly spew out of our mouths. We have all heard the stories of someone going postal. Such people always seem to have been good, quiet neighbors who never bothered anyone. This kind of suppression is no better than spilling our guts. Both have serious consequences. But if blurting or suppressing our toxic thoughts are both high-risk options, what are we left with?

Chris Argyris, formerly of Harvard Business School, developed a helpful exercise called the left-hand column. It's a simple yet powerful way to expose our private thoughts in conversation. The exercise invites the participant to document a recent conversation with some emotional charge. It could have been a conversation that left them feeling puzzled, frustrated, confused, angry, or passive. Or it could be a conversation that they will have soon that they are dreading. The more agonizing the conversation, the greater the learning potential. Be kind to yourself and remember that you likely didn't consciously choose your patterns of thought or your long-held opinions.

To start the left-hand column exercise, draw a vertical line down the middle of a piece of paper. Beginning with the right-hand column, try to create a verbatim transcript of the stressful conversation—"I said . . ." and "She said . . . ," as if someone has recorded the exchange. You're documenting the words that were spoken and the conversation's facts. Write four to six of the most emotionally charged exchanges for maximum benefit.

In the left-hand column, write what you were thinking and feeling in response to the words you wrote in the right-hand column. Include your thoughts and feelings—without editing anything. Include all of the nasty thoughts—the cursing, the judgments, the meanspirited slights. All of it. I know that sounds miserable, but getting them out of your head and on paper is one way to counter the noise in your head, and your ego's defenses. It is revealing and freeing.

○ ○

Antonio, the CFO of a major museum, and his sister Jane, a stay-at-home mom, talk over the phone about how best to take care of their eighty-four-year-old mother, who isn't well but is still living independently. They keep circling around the same points of contention, and they make little progress. They each have their story and no shortage of negative private thoughts. This ongoing conversation always leaves Antonio unsettled and frustrated with Jane. While working with me, he agrees to try the left-hand column exercise. Antonio sits down to write out the conversation as honestly as he possibly can (see table opposite).

First, in the right-hand column, he writes the actual words spoken. The spoken conversation sounds ordinary. On the surface, they kept their cool and sounded respectful and reasonable. But if we could have observed them during the conversation, their body language would have told a different story. They would have looked vexed and stressed. Unable to share their charged unspoken thoughts, Antonio and Jane were quietly steaming inside.

WHAT YOU WERE THINKING AND FEELING	WHAT YOU AND THE OTHER PERSON SAID
	Jane: "Can you please help out with Mom next week?"
	Antonio: "I don't know if I can make it next week to take care of Mom for all three days."
	Jane: "I know that you're super busy, but I think Mom needs to have someone here."
	Antonio: "Are the kids in school next week? Can you do it? That would work better for my schedule. Maybe I can do it for one day."
	Jane: "I'll think of something. Maybe I should start advertising for help."
	Antonio: "You know, I'm still not convinced that Mom needs someone full time."
	Jane: "We'll talk. Right now, I have to take her shopping."

Now Antonio warily moves to the second part of the exercise: writing what he was thinking and feeling during the conversation. Below are Antonio's private thoughts and feelings next to the words that he and his sister spoke in the right-hand column.

Here's Antonio's left-hand column:

WHAT YOU WERE THINKING AND FEELING	WHAT YOU AND THE OTHER PERSON SAID
Antonio: *Oh boy, here we go again! Jane's continuing saga.*	Jane: "Can you please help out with Mom next week?"
Antonio: *She's so clueless about how impossible it is for me to take a week off to help. She has all the time in the world.*	Antonio: "I don't know if I can make it next week to take care of Mom for all three days."
Antonio: *I can't believe you expect me to jeopardize my new project by taking care of Mom for a whole week!*	Jane: "I know you are super busy, but I think Mom needs to have someone here."
Antonio: *You have no idea how damn busy I am! Your kids are in school all day, and you don't work. You have so much free time on your hands that you stupidly obsess over Mom.*	Antonio: "Are the kids in school next week? Can you do it? Maybe I can do it for one day."
Antonio: *Oh, yeah. Here you go. Hiring help and spending what little money Mom has.*	Jane: "I'll think of something. Maybe I should start advertising for help."
Antonio: *You're not seeing this situation clearly. You're stressing like this is an emergency.*	Antonio: "You know, I'm still not convinced that Mom needs someone full time."
Antonio: *If you'd stop being a control freak, we could figure this out.*	Jane: "Let's talk again soon. Right now I have to take her shopping."

For Antonio, it was a revelation to see his private thoughts juxtaposed next to his public words. For most of us, seeing our negative judgments and stories in black and white is surprising and disconcerting. Have I mentioned how important it is to write this exercise down?

We might hear ourselves curse, judge, blame, and shame, but when we summon the courage to take a look under the hood, we can shift our thinking and transform conversations with colleagues, family, and friends. Rather than blurt them out or stuff them inside, in the next chapter we will process and transform them with the help of four archetypal questions.

PRACTICES

o Begin to notice the commentary of the committee running in the background of your mind.

o Notice the committee chatting away as you listen to the other person.

o When in conversation, take note of the ease or tension you feel based on the intensity of your private conversation.

o Pick a stressful or disappointing conversation about which you had an emotional reaction. Do a left-hand column exercise on paper.

> 1. On the right side of the paper, write exactly what you and the other person said (four or five exchanges). This is a transcript of the words spoken.
>
> 2. On the left side of the paper, write down what you were thinking and feeling about the words you spoke and the words the other person spoke.
>
> 3. Cultivate curiosity rather than judgment about your private thoughts.

4

PROCESSING OUR OPINIONS

Today I escaped from anxiety.
Or no, I discarded it, because it was within me,
in my own perceptions—not outside.

—MARCUS AURELIUS

This chapter introduces four archetypal questions that are key to deconstructing our opinions. Any one or any combination of the four questions can help us unearth our underlying feelings and thoughts. Throughout the book they will be a consistent guide for transforming all four conversations.

The process of refining petroleum products is a useful analogy for understanding the processing of our private conversations. Petroleum products are manufactured from raw crude oil and other liquids formed from animal and plant remains, which endured heat and pressure over millions of years, long before dinosaurs roamed Earth. The raw liquids are toxic and hazardous, but refined through distillation, they are converted into products that range from fuel to synthetic fabrics.

Unlike petroleum, a nonrenewable resource, our private conversations aren't ever going away. But like petroleum, our opinions and internal negative thoughts are toxic, haunting our minds and hampering our conversations. The good news is that like petroleum, our negative inner dialogue can be processed, and it can become surprisingly useful, although it takes practice to get to that point.

To harvest the good stuff, we must become a curious witness of our internal dialogue, detached from our thoughts and open to whatever the process might reveal. Our private thoughts are full of worries, dreams, judgments, and power issues.

Four quintessential elements constitute our opinions (see Figure 5). We can process our private conversation by asking four archetypal questions about them.

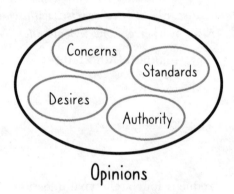

Opinions

FIGURE 5: Four quintessential elements of opinions

1. What are my desires?

In conversations, our desires lurk in the background of our minds. We're often unaware of the ways that desires can shape our opinions and judgments. They can be a major blind spot, locking us into unproductive conversations. Spinning or triggered, we can ask ourselves questions like: *What do I desire in this situation? What goals do I have? Am I attached to a particular outcome?* The questions expose gaps between our private thoughts and reality. When my desires are misaligned with reality, I suffer.

2. What are my concerns?

In working with others and facing tough issues, we all have concerns about what might happen. To bring to the fore your worries about the future, ask these questions: *What are my concerns? What worries are keeping me up at night?* You may be worried about what might go wrong, or you might simply not want tomorrow to end up like today. Our unconscious concerns are emotionally triggering and stressful. I have found that when I remember to share my concerns, the energy of a conversation can shift. Others can't deny my concerns, and the honesty creates space for them to safely voice theirs.

3. What power issues are at play?

In conversations, the question about authority is ubiquitous. Whether you're a leader, colleague, teacher, parent, or friend, issues of authority and control are always playing out, consciously and unconsciously. Human-made hierarchies grant varying types of authority to judges, priests, teachers, government officials, experts, and on and on. The authority to make business decisions, sports calls, government mandates, or scientific/ engineering recommendations are critical components of functioning society. As leaders, we can be conscious about how we use our power. As judges we can make decisions based on evidence and fairness. As parents, we have authority and responsibilities to teach our kids what's right and wrong, to keep them safe, and to let them discover their own voice and power. As friends, we tend to give some people's opinions more power while ignoring the opinions of others. For me, awareness of power issues is both freeing and empowering.

4. What rules and codes of conduct are shaping my opinions and judgments?

Our standards play an outsized and unappreciated role in our conversations. Each of our opinions, judgments, preferences, and prejudices are driven by the standards, morals, and scruples that we live by. Through our families and cultures, we adopt standards—consciously or unconsciously—of right or wrong, good or bad, pretty or ugly, smart or stupid, perfect or imperfect. Standards are the root of our tortured negative self-judgments and the critiques we hoist on others. When our standards go unexplored, our egos are fully in charge. We can be harsh on others, become indignant and righteous, and stand with disbelief toward others. When I remember to explore my standards, I can be less judgmental realizing that my standard is one of many.

The four questions help us understand the underbelly of our expressed and unexpressed or positive and negative opinions. Unexamined thoughts, assumptions, and judgments are responsible for most dysfunction in conversations with ourselves and with others.

When the four questions pair up with our work on emotions and facts, we can

○ Acknowledge our emotions and expose the stories behind them.

○ Mine the facts of any given situation.

○ Ask the four questions.

Before we take a closer look at the questions, let's consider how and why these critical elements are forgotten in our daily interactions.

The Background of Obviousness

Consciously and unconsciously, our desires, concerns, and standards—and to some extent, our power issues—operate in the background of our minds. Aligned with our stories, these elements are real and useful, but for the most part they operate on autopilot. *How could they not see that this project is doomed! Why would he think that I could ever act out that way? I can't believe they don't see that this design isn't going to make the cut.* What seems like a no-brainer to us is inaccessible information to others. The background of obviousness is a blinding conversational trap.

Parents wonder how their kids could think or behave so badly. Leaders forget to share context or important information with their employees, sending them to do work not fully briefed. Unspoken desires, undisclosed concerns, unclear standards, and concealed authority issues are all a part of miscommunications and misunderstandings. With that distinction in mind, let's take a closer look at the questions.

Desires

Our desires range from the seemingly simple (*I really want this conversation with the team to go well*) to emotion-laden (*I so want my kid to be accepted into Harvard*). What do we want? What are our goals? What aversions blind us? Our desires can serve us or stress us out. They're often hiding in the background of obviousness, but they are a consequential element of our opinions. Often our desires hide out in our dislikes and aversions. Desires and aversions are the opposite sides of what we think we want or don't want. Unexplored and undiscussed, they create anxiety and fear. Negative aversions have a power to grab our attention. Our thoughts say, *I hate how the team is paralyzed* or *He'll never stop treating me this way*. Although upsetting, they are important pointers to hidden desires (e.g., *I really want to turn this project around*, or *I'm ready for a better relationship*). Aversions can keep us stuck in a battle with reality (we can't believe what is happening) and our desires can keep us out of sync with reality (we want what we can't have). Unexamined, both can send us into a downward spiral.

At their best, desires are expressions of our goals and our dreams about the future. They serve us and tempt us, pushing us to do great work and helping us get through tough times. From day one, we begin to develop strong opinions about what we like, what we don't like, what we want to happen, and what we fear. We learn to effortlessly communicate those desires, saying such things as, "Yes, I've gotta have that!" or "No, I don't like that at all!" We're mostly unaware of the ways that our likes and dislikes become formidable thought patterns that influence what we feel and how we interact. At a young age, we innocently adopt innumerable desires and dislikes from our families and societies. Later, in adolescence, as we spread our wings, we often reject early desires and adopt others better aligned with our life. Constantly influenced by business or social standards, our likes and dislikes change as we grow. What attracts or repels us about relationships, food, clothing, art, romance, sports, and politics are the desires embedded in our opinions.

A basic premise of Buddhism is that our unexamined desires are the root of all human suffering. Although they can inspire our dreams, they also make us unhappy. We suffer when we don't get our way, can't understand why bad things happen, or resent life. Both desires and aversions can protect us or entrap us in fear. When we become more aware of both, we gain insights into our defended opinions, and we release the hold they have on us.

In Chapter 1, we discussed Paul, whose desire to get a promotion was an obsessive compulsion for him. Uninvestigated, his desire sent him into a downward spiral. He hated that others were (undeservedly) getting ahead of him, and his ego was eager to support his quest, protectively defending his unexamined desires and ignoring any facts. His excitement and expectations about an unknown future took hold, and he got stuck on autopilot. His desire to realize those expectations made him an emotional wreck. When he was ready to do his work and unravel his unrealistic expectations, he gained fresh perspectives and new choices for considering his future.

Now let's consider Tess, a mom of two young children whose looming decision about a new home and whose sincere desire to give her kids an excellent education is keeping her awake at night. She finds a perfect house with a great porch (something she has always wanted) in a neighboring town with excellent schools. Her husband, James, who is starting his software career, says that there's no way they can afford the house. Despite his protests, Tess finds herself driving by the house, muttering to herself, *So perfect . . . there has to be a way. Maybe I could get a part-time job to help pay for it! Why doesn't James make more money?*

Tess's desires have a firm grip on her. Her eager ego compels her to deny the facts of the situation. *It's such a great place with such good schools, and I've gotta have that porch!* Her storytelling brain conjures up a beautiful image of her whole family enjoying the porch on a summer evening, replete with rocking chairs, iced tea, and board games. Tess badly wants that house, and she thinks about it day and night. Frustrated and angry, she also feels powerless. Her private conversations run amok.

If Tess can catch herself spinning and investigate her story, she can step out of the drama and gain the perspective she needs to rethink the situation. By considering the facts of her story, she can discuss the family's financial realities with James. With undeniable numbers staring her in the face, she can begin to accept the reality of their financial situation. Though they are comfortable financially, the rent for the house Tess wants is a stretch. As Tess acknowledges and accepts their financial realities, she calms down and begins to examine the underbelly of her desires. As she becomes aware of her intense emotional desires related to the house, the porch, and the school, she recognizes how much stress those desires are causing her.

Her investigations loosen the firm grip of her unattainable desires. Thinking more clearly, she considers other options that allow her to satisfy some of her desires. Ultimately, a good education for her kids overrides the house's unrealistic attraction. Rather than focusing on what she can't do, she begins to research other school districts in more affordable towns, and she considers less costly rental options in those districts. She decides to hold on to her desire for a front porch in the future, but she doesn't let it sway her from finding good schools first. She has reframed her desires, set new goals, and found a clearer voice in this situation. She's ready to work with James to plan their future.

Facing our aversions and desires means waking up to what we like and loathe. When mindful, we can surface our desires from the background of our minds and consciously decide when they are serving us or harming us. We can unwind from their drama and shift out of autopilot. I now enjoy the times when I catch my desires spinning me down the funnel. I can have a good laugh at the gap between my expectations and the reality of the moment. I take a breath, wake up, and come back to Earth.

PRACTICES

o At work and at home, notice the desires that run in the background of your mind.

o Do you have any desires that are inspiring?

o Do you have desires that are at odds with reality and that set you spinning?

o In disappointing situations, ask yourself if a desire is at the root of your feelings.

Concerns

What are my concerns? What will tomorrow bring? Our concerns vary from minor worries to deep anxieties. There's *Yikes, is today's meeting still on?* or *Ugh, I'll never meet the deadline set for this project!* and then there's *Is this weird spot on my face skin cancer?* Although they may have a measure of fact in them (the deadline is four weeks away, and there is an odd spot on my face), our worries are our projections of what could happen. Worries can be obsessive, and they often stew in our private thoughts throughout the day. They too operate in the background of obviousness. When something is extra worrisome, it keeps us from being present and fills us with dread in the middle of the night.

When events or people trigger us, our brains quickly—with no effort on our part—generate assumptions and scary scenarios about what might happen tomorrow. Concerns are future-based. Part of this evolutionary brain pattern is useful, somewhat like having an inner coach whispering in our ear, "consider what the consequences of that decision might be." When concerns help us stay present or navigate trouble, they're useful. When they only present fretful scenarios, they send us spiraling down in fear of what might happen.

The ego is always ready to defend our worrisome private conversations. It says things like "This situation is going to play out badly, and when it does, you'll be screwed." To counter those negative conversations, we can start by asking ourselves a few questions: *What am I worried about? What am I afraid will happen? What fretful story am I telling myself about the future? What are the facts in real time? In this moment am I okay?*

Consider Rodney, a successful executive and a naturally anxious guy. He's enjoying a long-deserved vacation on a beautiful remote beach that is accessible only via a regional commuter train. After a few days of winding down, he learns from a local fisherman that a hurricane is due to make landfall in two days. Rodney's inner dialogue has him freaking out. His private thoughts are full of floods, winds, storm surges, destruction, and death—specifically his. His anxiety goes into overdrive, and his thoughts spin downward. He generates a story about his need to get out of town as soon as possible. He hikes a few miles to town, seeking escape. He pleads and yells at ticket sellers, making a scene, only to learn that the train is booked for the next two days.

Had Rodney caught himself spinning, he might have come to his senses and asked a few calming questions. Had Rodney taken a breath and collected a few facts, he would have learned that the exact location where the storm would hit was unpredictable. That could have helped him unlock from his gotta-get-out-of-here-now story. Whatever the level of our anxiety, in any stressful situation, it's good to stop and examine our concerns. When we acknowledge them, we stop making awful predictions about the future, and we can find some clarity in the moment. If Rodney had assessed his concerns, he could have calmed down and thought more clearly about the situation.

Now let's meet Carla, an easygoing woman vacationing at the same hotel where Rodney is staying. When she runs into him in the lobby and says hi, she notices his stress and agitation. In a friendly, caring voice she asks, "Are you worried about the storm? What are you concerned about?" After hearing his story, she tells him, "Today I talked to a few locals about how they prepare for storms. They gave me some good advice."

At first, Rodney is so stressed and stuck that he can't hear what Carla says, and he dismisses her. Later he decides to find Carla and see what she has to say. It turns out that she got some important info from the locals. They stay tuned to the weather updates, and when a storm comes their way, they know how and where to hunker down for safety. Carla befriends Rodney, and together they track the storm with the locals. Carla's calm approach and simple questions about Rodney's concerns are enough to bring him to his senses.

When we're stressed out, concerns are often the easiest and most calming elements of our stories to unearth. They can reveal whether our worries are fact or fiction and allow us to determine whether we're negatively projecting into the future. A few good questions bring them to the light so we can manage our emotions with a few facts and rational ideas about our next moves.

PRACTICES

o Notice concerns that have you fretting day and night.

o Note whether there are patterns to your worries.

o Pay attention to how your concerns relate to time. Are they projections into an unknown future? How do they relate to your desires?

o What are the facts about a stressful situation that could help you reduce your worries and be more present in the moment?

o Notice how your emotions shift when you acknowledge and process your concerns.

Authority

In many of our opinions, authority issues carry a hidden, powerful punch. Who has what authority and in what context? What power issues are at play?

One way or another, we often give or deny power to someone in our daily interactions at work and at home, and we often unknowingly give away our power to others and don't claim our rightful authority.

When we hold someone in high esteem and believe they are capable, smart, and successful, we unconsciously assign some level of power and authority to their words and actions. We might simply follow their lead, or we might meekly agree with their positions. Conversely, when we believe that someone is dimwitted or inadequate, we don't grant their words any authority. Consciously or unconsciously, minute by minute, we give or deny power to the words and actions of others.

We also grant or deny authority to ourselves. Our internal beliefs about our strengths and weaknesses determine how we talk about and present ourselves. Unconsciously, we have self-limiting, power-based stories about ourselves, and our private conversations can be jammed with self-limiting, power-related opinions. When my father and grandfather told me that I wasn't a "big enough man," I innocently gave their opinions tons of authority. When I was a child, those powerful negative voices sank in and subconsciously minimized my voice and limited my behavior.

Power plays out informally (e.g., social interactions) and formally (e.g., hierarchies or assigned authority). Social rules and cultural patterns of authority—subtle and blatant—are how businesses are organized, how we relate to friends and family, and how the military keeps soldiers in line. In business and politics, authority is formally assigned to individuals and institutions. We assign authority to police, politicians, captains, doctors, referees, and judges. This gives them the power to make decisions, legal arrests, and rules we live by. It's a crucial structure of civil societies. Although authority is present in all aspects of society, it often operates in the background of our awareness. It serves us well and has many benefits based on our human inclinations toward fairness. Power in the hands of a self-aware person can inspire, and there's no shortage of leaders, judges, or teachers that use their authority fairly in service of others, but, as Michael Lewis explores in his podcast *Against the Rules*, how life gets refereed is an important function that is dying a slow death as authority and facts are questioned or disrespected. Authority in the hands of power hungry, egotistical, abusive, or racist individuals is socially disruptive and runs counter to our innate sense of fairness.

In nature, hierarchies rule. Eat or be eaten is the basic principle. In societies, hierarchies serve a purpose, ranging from egalitarian to repressive. We rely on them to organize and get things done. Ignoring, blaming, or denying hierarchies won't make them go away. But when we're more mindful of their impact, we can live and act wisely within them.

Authority and hierarchies are neither inherently good nor inherently bad. They can be rigid or fluid, fair or unfair, clear or confusing, and helpful or hindering. Well-defined hierarchies help groups of people make decisions and accomplish tasks in efficient and effective ways. When blessed with talented leadership, hierarchies can empower people. Well-delineated, fair, and respectful hierarchies produce success and bring about powerful change.

It's enlightening to examine our personal power issues, and it can be surprising to discover how we use or abuse our personal authority. Investigating it reveals our stories about power. I couldn't undo the story that I had internalized about masculinity from my grandfather until I was a grown man. When I examined the story and acknowledged the facts, I could see how my personal power was diminished. Once I'd investigated it, the story ceased to have power over me. When I dropped it, I felt as though a weight had been lifted from my shoulders. I was affected physically and psychologically. Weeks later, I was having coffee with my partner when my height registered in my psyche for the first time. I thought, *Damn, I'm taller than this guy.*

Modern hierarchies don't determine our likelihood of survival, as they did for our ancestors on the savannah, but our unconscious and conscious rankings of self and others and our private judgments about authority create consequences that range from productively powerful to tremendously destructive. When we hold strong negative stories about authority, we suffer. They can be unconscious, self-oriented, fear-based, and harmful. In such cases, we might react and speak with an inappropriately arrogant degree of authority. That's when we become so invested in being right that we're unaware of the negative impact it has on others. We can also find ourselves on the receiving end of this dynamic. The power of our parents' voices, a boss's commands, or our colleagues' criticisms reverberate deep inside us. In our relationships at work and home, there's no shortage of authority and power issues quietly driving our behavior in the background.

Take Paul, for example. His ego was totally convinced that he deserved a promotion to director in his department. He wanted it badly, and he stressed about it. But with a little coaching, Paul took some time to consider what authority issues could be part of his distress. With a few questions about the hierarchy of his work environment, he realized for the first time that he had very limited power and control over his future with his company. As is true in most hierarchies, Paul could control the quality of his work, but he ultimately had no control over the decisions made about his future. This realization was a check on the dreams of his ego.

To examine our patterns of thought around power, we should ask these questions: *What issues of authority are at play? Where do I rebel against authority? If socially assigned power is unfair (e.g., police, priests, community leaders, politicians), can I fight against them to assure equality and civil decency? When do I use my power to inappropriately exploit others? How do I behave with my kids, colleagues, or bosses when unconscious reactions to authority trip me up or trap me in unhealthy relationships?* In stressful situations, we can examine our private conversations and explore how authority dynamics are playing out. Here are the most common dynamics:

○ There's no way they will listen to me (insecurity).

○ I don't think I'm getting what I deserve (control).

○ Her idea will win because she has the CFO twisted around her finger (hierarchies).

○ No worries. I have this totally covered (confidence or arrogance).

All these answers reveal hidden power issues that play out unconsciously in our unexplored opinions. The more we investigate issues of power, the more we can appropriately claim our rightful authority and grant others theirs.

Ultimately, power is about boundaries and control. Spiritual teacher Byron Katie has helped me accept what I have and what I can and can't change. She recognizes a useful distinction between three types of power. In our minds, whose business are we in—God's business, other people's business, or our business? So our questions about power are about boundaries and patterns of control. Are we truly honest about what we can and can't control? Are we stressed because we're in someone else's business and we have little chance of accomplishing anything besides feeding our ego? Are we angry because we're in God's business and don't have a chance in hell of changing the reality in front of us?

There are endless opportunities to see our egos at work, defending our perspectives while issues of power quietly reside in the background of obviousness. When we take a conscious look, we can manage issues of power in constructive ways. In any conversation, if we feel off center, we can listen to our intuitions and ask ourselves the authority question. I have experienced conversations where my body signals a bit of fear and a turn down the funnel. *Is this person's oppositional position oppressive? Are they pulling a power play? Am I shrinking away from articulating my position with passion and making a case with facts, concerns, and goals?* These questions are a circuit-breaker moment. Asking myself these questions, I can assess the interactions, regain my center, and reengage in the conversation with more self-assurance and clarity. Best-case scenario, the shift in how I engage can reset the relationship and change the energy of most conversations.

I have also been in conversations in which I was hooked on my perspective and promoted it forcefully. This is another way to catch ourselves spiraling down and wake up in the moment. Aware of issues of power, I was attuned to when others weren't speaking up and the conversation was feeling dead. As I caught my overpowering posture in real time, I could consciously shift the conversation by zipping up my lips and asking to hear from others.

Another type of issue with authority is in conversations when unproductive or imbalanced power rules. This can be a business meeting or a social setting in which one leader's or one person's ego is consciously or unconsciously presenting their perspective as the "right and only" one. In that context, most of us can shrink back and go quiet to avoid conflict. As we become aware of issues of power, we can recognize these dynamics. We summon a bit of courage, and without confronting the culprit, we can speak up. "I'd like to hear other perspectives in the room. I'm curious if we all have the same goal in mind or if we all have the same concerns about where this is going."

Authority and power are pervasive in all conversations. As we pay more attention to their benefits and pitfalls, we're more likely to know when and where to productively empower ourselves and others to speak up.

PRACTICES

o At work and at home, start being curious about issues of authority.

o When triggered, take note of your unconscious feelings or patterns of thought regarding authority.

o Note particular circumstances where power is a trigger.

- Note if particular kinds of people trigger authority/power issues for you. Where or how do you use authority, consciously and unconsciously?

- Are there situations in which your ego digs in its heels and is righteous about being right?

- Are there areas in your life in which you don't claim your power in a productive way?

Standards

Standards are the measuring sticks of our stories' opinions. *What rules and codes of conduct are shaping my opinions and judgments?*

They operate in the background of almost all conversations, and they can have major consequences. When we tell tales about why a leader's behavior is rotten, about how useless a meeting is, or about how great that three-point shot was, our standards are operating in the background of obviousness. But standards determine how we think things should or shouldn't be, what we believe to be right or wrong, and what we should or shouldn't do. Words, leadership, missions, behavior, weather, goals, sex, work, parenting, religion—nothing escapes our standards. We always have a good story about how and why things could/couldn't, would/wouldn't, or should/shouldn't be.

As we ask the standards question (or any of the other questions), we should set aside our automatic judgments and be gentle with ourselves. Standards are the foundations of our moral compasses, but we mostly didn't consciously choose them. We adopt our standards based on the culture, society, and families we live in. There's no shortage of standards that we unconsciously and consciously maintain about subjects, big and small. Reflecting on our standards helps us unhook from their grip, arrest our autopilot reactions, and choose to change them.

Shared and transparent, our standards keep society humming along. They help us live together civilly. They are vital for reducing conflict.

In democracies, we live by the standard known as the *rule of law*. Constitutions, laws, mission statements, cultural norms, rules of diplomacy, business contracts, and instruction manuals are just a few of the standards that organize our communities. Other forms of government (e.g., communism) have very different standards, which seem abhorrent to some of us, but for those born into those systems, they feel quite normal. No matter where we live, individuals, families, organizations, and nations are held accountable by their community standards.

The bad news is that the extreme variability and pervasiveness of standards can quickly set us at odds with others. They are ripe territory for righteous egos, stoking conflicts related to *musts* and *shoulds*. Standards are how we defend and prove that we're right and others are wrong. They are the ego's idea of heaven. Our standards are so inherent to how we define ourselves that when they are tested or challenged, we can start spinning without being aware we are doing so.

○ ○

Gabrielle lives in Chicago and works for a large organization whose parking policy mandates that the closest, most convenient, non-handicapped parking spaces should be reserved for visitors, not employees. Each day, Gabrielle abides by the policy, like a good employee should—she's a rule-keeper. Even on frigid winter mornings, she trudges from the far end of the parking lot, past the visitor spaces, and into the lobby. On several cold days, she notices that Michael, the chief financial officer (CFO), has parked his car in a space marked "Visitors Only." On the fourth day, she goes into a tailspin, and she becomes obsessed with this blatant rule-buster. Her private story grumbles, *Who does he think he is? He must think he's special.*

On day five, she sees Michael in the lobby, forces a smile, and says, "Hi, Michael. Nice car right outside. Is it new?" Meanwhile she's thinking, *Aren't you embarrassed to have your shiny new car parked in the visitor spot?* Gabrielle has quite a gap between her private and public conversations. If she were to investigate her private conversation, she would recognize her frustration and anger.

She's steaming, but she takes a breath and decides to do some exploring. What are the facts of her story? Michael's brand-new car has been parked in a visitor spot for several days. It's only twenty degrees outside, and she's parked at the farthest corner of the employee parking lot. It's only 8 A.M., and she's already stressed.

Gabrielle writes down her judgments: "The company has a rule that applies to all employees, so, geez, it should apply to *all* employees, even the CFO. It should be fair and equitable!" Her ego wants to defend her desire for fairness, and her disdain for power affects her emotions. Gabrielle notices her spin, so she decides to slow down and ask herself a few questions.

She probes her standards. She believes that employees, from the CEO to the janitor, should be held to the same standards. Gabrielle's standards and story have her in a battle with reality. It's a fact that the CFO has parked in the visitor's space for several days. She doesn't like it, and she imagines that he's parked there because he believes that his privilege entitles him to that comfort.

Still frustrated but less angry, she decides to ask someone in security about the parking space rules and the CFO's car. A security guard politely informs her that the CFO has a temporary disability and has a short-term handicap sticker on his license. As she's walking back to her office, she's surprised and, in a funny way, relieved. The stress of the situation and her judgments kicked her into a spin that dropped her to the bottom of the funnel. In her rage, she never noticed the handicap placard hanging in his car. Her story, with all its judgmental standards and distrust of authority, was blinding.

o o

When Gabrielle investigated her feelings and the facts and asked the four questions, she discovered that multiple parts of her private conversation had been driving her emotions. If she had checked her automatic emotional reactions on the first day she saw him parked in the spot, when her anger was just starting to brew, she could have spared herself several days of rage. As Gabrielle explores her thoughts, she becomes conscious of her standards and of the intensity of her feelings and private conversations. She's relieved and has a good laugh at herself as she learns a life lesson.

In our minds, our standards are perfectly rational, while others' standards can seem incomprehensible. When they're unclear, badly articulated, enforced unjustly, or interpreted differently, they will, without fail, send us into battle. They are a ruling force, often in partnership with issues of authority, in passionate disputes within families, teams, communities, and governments. Take any hot-button topic in the news, and we can see standards and accompanying authority issues lurking in the shadows. Though strongly felt, they are often unexpressed.

As we pay attention to standards, we will see them playing a role in discombobulated interactions. In business, I routinely see disagreements over ideas, products, or decisions. Lisa is a good example. She's a high-profile engineer, who holds very high standards for defining success or value of an idea or decision. Her standard is based on facts and physics. *Is this physically possible? Can we engineer the parts to achieve our desired outcome?* Lisa's standard isn't a secret. Anyone working for her knows the standard by which all ideas, processes, and decisions will be measured. Some can't survive the rigor of this standard and move on, but those who can cope eventually outperform less rigorous engineers.

On many teams, standards are never discussed. Leaders who are blind to the standards they hold suffer from the background of obviousness. What looks good to them should look good to all. With standards out of a conversation, assumptions and misunderstandings prevail.

Imagine how things might change if politicians had common goals and could actually agree on the standards for establishing a new law. If they agreed on minimizing inequality, setting specific standards for minimum wages, supporting childcare, and increasing job opportunities, they would have a solid foundation to build from. Bringing standards to the forefront of our conversations can provide a focus for challenges in business, families, and social communities.

PRACTICES

o Jot down a few strong judgments that send you spinning. Ask yourself what standards are lurking in the
background.

o Notice what standards show up on a regular basis.

o Notice how your unconscious standards drive immediate
judgments.

o How do your feelings change when you recognize your
standards as standards and not as the only way to think
about a given subject?

o Are there other standards at work or at home that you're
willing to reassess?

Our opinions and private conversations are a powerful duo. With
the four questions, we can get to the underbelly of our thinking with
less judgment and trouble-making assumptions. We don't give up our
stories, but when we bring them to the light of awareness, we can shift
our attitude and enter into conversations humbly. We can then share
our desires, concerns, and standards with an open hand rather than a
clenched fist. This crucial work is a prerequisite for successful collaborating conversations.

PRACTICES

Pick one or more stressful conversations you have strong opinions about, then ask yourself:

o *What emotions am I feeling in this situation?*

o *What are the facts? Am I fighting something I have no control over or an event that can't be changed?*

o *Are standards driving my negative reactions?*

o *What are my concerns? Am I projecting into the future?*

o *What unconscious issues of authority or power might be playing out?*

o *What are my desires? Are they misaligned with reality?*

Part II

COLLABORATIVE CONVERSATIONS
Seek to Understand and Absorb Other Perspectives

IN CONVERSATIONS WITH OTHERS

Synergy: The combined effect of individuals in collaboration that exceeds the sum of their individual effects.

—STEPHEN COVEY

tories, facts, egos, emotions, and strong opinions are the ingredients of conversations. When those dynamic ingredients intersect and conflict, collaborative conversations are challenging. The personal work of understanding and transforming our stories is a prerequisite for creating productive collaborations. Our investigations open our eyes and ears to new ways to see, hear, and engage with others.

When I busted my big-enough-man story, the lingering doubt that I wouldn't or couldn't measure up slowly evaporated. As I became aware of my stories as one of many possible stories and not the truth, I could practice being less judgmental of others. Slowly, I was able to tune in with curiosity, understanding, and empathy.

Stories and the many ways they manifest are what make or break collaborative conversations. Every person in the room has at least one story to tell. When multiple stories sync up, our conversations feel easy. We connect, agree, and find common ground, and collaboration feels seamless. But when our stories, egos, and different perspectives clash, collaboration takes a back seat to criticism, defensive arguments, and a host of emotions. While seamless collaboration feels good and heated interactions feel bad, neither option makes for successful collaborative conversation.

Aligned stories can lock out fresh ideas and are often the product of groupthink or a power imbalance. They skip over the give and take of surfacing and considering different perspectives and the surprise of unexpected solutions. A conversation in a room full of people with aligned stories might sound something like this:

Drake, the leader: *"Let's get this meeting started."*

"This one's easy. We all agree on the fix, right?"

Robin: *"I am so ready to kick this project into high gear."*

Kate: *"What's not to love about this solution?"*

Drake: *"OK, Decision made. What's next?"*

Clashing stories, on the other hand, leave little room for listening, understanding opposing positions, and creating solutions. Those conversations sound like this:

"Morning. Coffee ready?"

"We're out of coffee, and I can't drive the kids to school. My boss needs me for a last-minute meeting."

"Jesus, I can't do it all! Your job is going to kill me. For just this morning, can you put your boss off and help out?!"

"What's your problem this morning?"

Appreciating the hold that stories and opinions have on us, we can begin to understand how easily collaborative conversations can go awry. They can turn a happy morning into a steaming exchange or rush us into a lousy decision. But both extremes—groupthink and hardened defensive interactions—can be avoided by practicing purposeful collaborative conversations.

Most likely we experience both extremes on a daily basis without much thought. Sometimes conversations hum along without a hitch, and life is good. Other times an interaction goes off the rails, and we spiral down. With the help of a few tools—processing our private thoughts in conversation with others, open advocacy and inquiry, and mindful listening—we can create productive collaborative conversations.

Here's an example of how our skill (or lack thereof) in engaging in collaborative conversations can affect teams.

First-Quarter Fiasco

Susan is a software engineer working as director of a new and highly visible product development project at a major American technology company in the US. She and five of her colleagues report to a senior vice president, Eric, who is in charge of the project. The mission is critical for the company, and timelines and budgets are tight. Eric sets high standards, and he knows that the team must embrace transparent, non-siloed communication to get the job done.

After the first-quarter reviews of the project's goals, Eric begins to get feedback that Susan isn't fully cooperating with her colleagues and is often stepping on the toes of their direct reports. Her colleagues' emotions range from mildly concerned to pissed off. As Eric investigates this dysfunction, he learns that Susan withholds data from her colleagues, plays politics, and doesn't focus on the team's priorities. Her behavior and inability to collaborate successfully run counter to the team's mission, and the team's progress slows down. Susan was blind to the consequences of her behavior, and her colleagues didn't know how to give her constructive feedback. Their struggles could go on and on because they couldn't have a collaborative conversation.

○ ○

Not knowing how to have collaborating conversations sends teams and families into downward spirals. The collaborative conversation tools build on the work of processing toxic thoughts and managing our ego and emotions. Those skills come in handy as we practice advocating for ourselves and others and asking good questions to find common ground. The skills and tools of this section can dramatically shift seemingly immovable interactions toward respectful and productive dialogue.

While these conversations are complicated, our defensive patterns play an oversized role in how they unfold. Most—if not all—of these frustrating conversations result from uninvestigated stories. Adverse emotional reactions go undetected or hidden; we go a bit wacky; we experience hurt, anger, disappointment; and our fight-or-flight-or-freeze responses kick in. When multiple people are stuck in their stories, it is like a collision of spinning tops.

It's helpful to remember that our patterned responses in conversation with others are a product of our senses, our social norms, our emotional palate, and our beliefs. These well-worn response patterns are one reason collaboration can feel so difficult. Our habits, patterns, and stories are like old friends: comforting and easy to be with. Collaboration asks us to step out of our comfort zone so we can participate in robust dialogue. At its best, the tools of the collaborative conversation help us engage with an open mind and heart.

○ ○

A major kink in our ability—or inability—to effectively collaborate is the private, unrecognized troublemaking thoughts we explored in Chapters 3 and 4. We often find ourselves wrestling with or becoming distracted by our inner thoughts during a conversation. While being polite, we might be thinking, *Is she intentionally trying to piss me off?* Or we might say, "Okay, sure, I get it," while thinking, *I honestly have no idea what the hell you're talking about.* We simply can't listen, absorb, or seek compromise when our inner dialogue is running on autopilot.

A good example is the way we struggle in disbelief when someone is telling us about how triumphant they feel at an event that outraged us (think of the 2016 and 2020 presidential elections). Or how we feel when a colleague dismisses us in a meeting with the boss. In most frustrating interactions, the guilty culprits are unprocessed private conversations and unexplored conflicting interpretations.

In our interactions, we aren't transmitting and receiving data like TVs and radios—signal sent, signal received. Unlike radio antennae, our reception of others' words is rarely straightforward because of our big, beautiful, filtering, sense-making brain. When a friend, colleague, or stranger says, "Do you believe that?" within milliseconds your interpretation of their words plays out in your mind. Whether it's person-to-person conversations, emails, text messages, or phone calls, our interpretations are rarely 100 percent on the money. What we say isn't what someone else hears, and what someone else says isn't what we hear.

A healthy collaborative conversation requires more of us. We can hold our stories lightly, and learn to ask questions; we can seek to understand and not be afraid of collaboration's dynamic give-and-take. With practice, we become better witnesses of ourselves and a roomful of opinions. When we step out of autopilot practice and catch our reactions, how we interact with others shifts. Collaborative conversations ask us to advocate for our perspective as an opinion rather than fact: "Here's what I'm thinking." Or "I think it's possible the deadline can be moved by two weeks." And one person asking a few good questions can shift a contentious conversation into a mutually beneficial interaction. "How does that sound to you all?" Or, "Are there other way of thinking about this that we're missing?"

To be better collaborators, we return to processing our private thoughts and take a look at their role in our interactions with others.

PRACTICES

o   Notice how others present their opinions. Do you hear them as the truth? Do you grant authority to their opinions?

o   Pay extra attention to the way that facts and opinions are bandied about in conversations. Note if opinions rule and facts lurk in the background.

o   Note how you present your opinions. Is your tone bullying, humble, accusatory?

o   Are your opinions charged and judgmental?

o   In conversations take note of how facts and opinions intertwine indistinguishably.

PRIVATE CONVERSATIONS

*Remember that stress doesn't come
from what's going on in your life.*

*It comes from your thoughts about
what's going on in your life.*

—ANDREW J. BERNSTEIN,
American philosopher and author of
The Capitalist Manifesto

n Chapter 3, we deconstructed our stories to become aware of our private thoughts. In this chapter, we consider what happens when multiple private/public conversations between two or more people intersect. Once again, the four questions become our guide and help us make our case, seek to understand others, and take some of the mystery out of fractious interactions. We can ask questions like these: "What are the different ways to think about this issue?" "Can we agree on any facts?" "What concerns do we have?" "How do we measure success?" and "Who has the authority to make a decision?" These clear the way so that unspoken fears and worries can surface.

○ ○

In the "First-Quarter Fiasco" example in Chapter 5, unresolved and unspoken differences sent the team into downward spirals. Eric, Susan, and her colleagues were all caught up in their private interpretations of the team's shenanigans. There were clear goals, standards, and reporting structures, so what was missing? Susan's ego, her "my team"-centric behavior, and her power plays triggered the spiral. In meetings with her colleagues, her unchecked attitude and her colleagues' fearful reluctance to speak bred dysfunction. Eric's leadership style—his hesitancy and inability to give Susan productive negative feedback—prolonged that dysfunction. Unspoken concerns went underground, and undiscussables festered, stoking resentment and anger.

Skillful feedback rooted in facts, concerns, and standards of behavior would have given Susan an opportunity to change her attitude and behavior. A healthy, honest team conversation—wherein they agreed on a common goal, surfaced their concerns, and established shared standards—could have dramatically reshaped the team's dynamics and its culture.

As we discussed in Chapter 3, the wider the gap between our public words and our private thoughts, the more stress we experience. In challenging conversations with others, awareness of our private thoughts helps us see that our partner, colleague, friend, or lover also has their fair share of them. Over time, we can become more empathetic to other people's struggles. Whenever I'm unfairly judgmental, I remind myself of this quote from Plato: "Be kind, for everyone you know is fighting a hard battle."

Aware or not, we are constantly telegraphing our thoughts and emotions through our eyes, body language, and tone of voice. We are all walking advertisements of what we are thinking and feeling. In every interaction, myriad clues subtly telegraph our private conversations and without conscious attention, we are blind to contradictory messages we are broadcasting.

Ironically, when we entertain our negative, unfiltered thoughts, we get a hit of dopamine. *That'll teach that arrogant bastard.* Or, *She'll never do that again!* But when spoken aloud, they sting. They feel cruel; they make us feel hurt, angry, or disappointed, and we slide down the spiral, feeling rejected and unloved. Thoughtless unfiltered words always lead to crappy consequences.

Two days later, we can wake up out of autopilot and realize the harm we have done. We regret what we said, and we wish we could hit the rewind button and find a better way to speak our truths. Most of us have also experienced that uncomfortable moment when hurtful or accusatory words slip out of our mouths.

Unprocessed (spoken or unspoken) negative thoughts affect individuals, relationships, and our work and actions with others. In Susan's case, each colleague was upset and spun up about her politics. Eric was tied in knots, unable to help his team. The team dynamics got worse and worse over the course of a few months. Silent rumors distracted the team, and distrust began to seep into their interactions. Their work suffered, and progress toward their deadline slowed.

There are many reasons why it's hard to honestly assess our inner thoughts—fear of being wrong, an aversion to confrontation, defensiveness, contempt for the other, patterns of avoidance, or being overwhelmed. Our secrets and unexpressed emotions manifest as disappointment, frustration, confusion, disillusionment, resentment, and resignation, and nothing good comes from them. All that stress has health consequences—physical (e.g., high blood pressure, tight muscles, obesity, and sweaty palms) and psychological (e.g., anxiety, sadness, irritability, restlessness, and depression). Witnessing our negative inner thoughts and transforming them is our best shot for discovering the golden nuggets they hold.

As a mediator in civil court cases in Massachusetts, I had the privilege of working with people involved in family, social, or contractual conflicts. In mediation, there are always two or more conflicting stories, and there's plenty of blame and shame to go around. And there's no shortage of unprocessed private conversations. As a mediator, I witnessed the pain and the passion underlying many people's stories.

Ideally, a successful mediator is neutral, present, and open-minded. The following is an example that demonstrates how the four questions, guided by curiosity and openness, can help conflicted parties understand their own stories and the stories of their adversaries. With willing participants, the process builds bridges of understanding and can dissolve recalcitrant differences.

The mediation in this example involves a mother, Adrienne, and her son, Sammy. After multiple screaming arguments, they weren't speaking, and social services notified Sammy that he was headed for juvenile detention. The process started with separate meetings with Adrienne and Sammy, where they could safely tell their stories.

A mediator listens and acknowledges stories, seeks facts, and calms emotions. As the mediator builds trust, the participants relax and become more open to good questions that can help them unwind and disentangle the situation by revealing their private thoughts. They might then be able to consider their adversaries' feelings. We meet when both parties are ready and willing—sometimes after multiple rounds of individual meetings—to hear the other person and to seek resolution.

I'm condensing this mediation process and highlighting the four questions in the name of brevity.

○ ○

Adrienne and her son, Sammy, came into mediation with clenched fists, and they were barely able to look at one another. First, I met with Sammy. Here's the short version of what we said in the mediation session:

Me: *"What's been happening between you and your mom? What did you do or say? What did your mom do or say?" (In other words, what are the facts?)*

Sammy: *"Well, I kicked in the stupid basement door 'cause I couldn't stand to live with my mom anymore 'cause she's always on my butt. She constantly harasses me." (Authority)*

Me: *"That sounds tough. What was she on your butt about?" (Facts)*

Sammy: *"Do this! Do that! It's always something. I can't do anything right." (Standards)*

Me: *"So your frustration has been building, then you kicked in the door. What were you feeling at that moment?" (Emotions)*

Sammy: *"I can't win, and if she found out that I was smoking pot down in the basement, she would have totally blown up. I shouldn't have lost it and kicked in the door, but I'd just had it with the nagging."*

Me: *"Are you willing to meet with me and her so we can find a better way forward?" (Desires) "We can all talk to see if you can agree on some new rules." (Standards)*

Sammy: *"Yeah. I don't want to end up in juvenile detention."*

Me: *"Are you willing to tell her how you felt and to hear her out? Perhaps we can find some things you can both do so you can live together more peacefully." (Standards)*

Sammy: *"I am willing to help out, but only if the nagging stops."*

Me: *"Can I talk to your mom about our conversation?"*

Sammy: *"Sure."*

After my meeting with Sammy, I met with Adrienne, knowing how Sammy felt and what he was willing to do. Getting Sammy to agree to allow me to talk with his mom was key to building bridges of understanding. Here's the short version of what Adrienne and I said in our meeting:

Me: *"Sounds like things between you and your son have been rocky. What happened that led you to mediation?"*

Adrienne: *"I don't know. He seems angry with me all the time. Just last week, he kicked in the basement door and stormed off in a rage."*

Me: *"That must have been scary. What was happening when he kicked in the door?" (Facts)*

Adrienne: *"I just asked him to clean up his room, then he lost it."*

Me: *"What were you feeling or thinking at that moment?" (Private thoughts)*

Adrienne: *"I felt disrespected! I'm his mom, and I need him to do what I ask. Isn't that my job?"* (Authority)

Me: *"So, you want him to do chores and help around the house?"* (Desires)

Adrienne: *"Yes, but he fights me about anything I ask him to do."* (Authority)

Me: *"In my conversation with Sammy, he told me that he feels like you're constantly nagging him. Is that how it feels to you?"*

Adrienne: *"I guess I can see why he thinks that, but he rarely does what I ask him to do. He needs to help out."*

Me: *"In my conversation with him, I heard how scared he is of juvenile detention. He's willing to talk to see if you can agree on some new rules so you can live together."* (Standards) *"How does that sound to you?"*

Adrienne: *"Maybe, but it sure seems like he doesn't want to do anything. And I know that he's smoking pot in the basement. I don't know what I'm doing wrong."* (Concerns)

Me: *"He was very concerned that you would find out about the pot. How do you feel about that?"*

Adrienne: *"I mostly object to it being in the house, stinking up the place. I have concerns, but if he's going to do it, I'd prefer that he did it outside."*

Me: *"Can I bring that up when we meet together?"*

Adrienne: *"Okay."*

Me: *"So, it's okay with you for the three of us to meet to see if you come to an agreement about how to move forward?"*

Adrienne: *"That's fine. I'll hope for the best."*

During these one-on-one meetings, people enter with anger, resentment, and resignation. Their stories are hot with blame and shame. A critical role for a mediator is listening without judging, acknowledging people's stories and pain, and asking good questions to open minds and hearts. When it works (and it always feels miraculous), it's like letting the air out of a balloon ready to pop. Each person becomes a bit more relaxed, vulnerable, open to their adversaries' thoughts and feelings and to possible solutions.

With Adrienne's and Sammy's permission, we had a three-way conversation.

> Me: *"Thanks for agreeing to meet with one another. Sounds like both of you would like to find a way to move forward with less anger and stress. Is that true for you, Adrienne?"* (Desires, Goals)

> Adrienne: *"Yes, that would be good. But I need him to do his part."*

> Me: *"And Sammy?"*

> Sammy: *"I can help if she stops the constant nagging."*

> Adrienne: *"Sammy, I'm sorry about the nagging. I just didn't know how to get you to help without asking. If we can agree on your chores, that would be a great start."*

> Me: *"Okay, let's explore. Adrienne, what ideas do you have?"*

> Adrienne: *"There are three chores I'd like your help with: taking out the garbage and recycling, putting your dirty clothes in a bin instead of the floor, and washing the dishes, whether we eat together or you eat alone. Oh, and if you're gonna smoke pot, please do it outside!"*

> Sammy: *"Who told you about the pot?!"*

> Adrienne: *"Sammy, I wasn't born yesterday. When you smoke inside, it stinks up the house."*

> Sammy: *"Wow, I didn't even know you knew."*

Me: *"How do these things sound to you, Sammy?"*

Sammy: *"I'm willing to try helping more if she'll get off my back."*

Me: *"What about the three things your mom is asking about?"*

Sammy: *"Okay, I'll give it a try. Can she stop nagging?"*

Adrienne: *"Sammy, if you can do these things, I'll have less reason to nag."*

Sammy: *"That would be great!"*

Me: *"Let's work out some specifics about what you both can agree to do moving forward."*

As the session continued, we wrote down specific rules for moving forward. Sammy and Adrienne both felt hopeful and agreed to make it work. When the parties of mediation acknowledge each other's concerns and feelings, egos quiet down and emotions cool off. There's space in the conversation for mutual empathy and understanding, and the energy of the conversation shifts and moves things forward.

The questions about what happened, about the rules, about the lack of respect, and about what's possible led Adrienne and Sammy to feel and think about the situation in a new way. Slowly but surely, they exposed their feelings, became more vulnerable, and shifted their awareness. The process helped them unearth a few golden nuggets, like Adrienne's concerns about the smell of pot in the house and Sammy's fear of juvenile detention. Bit by bit, they could rebuild their relationship and engage one another more openly and respectfully.

○ ○

The main benefit of mediation is that a neutral party guides the work of detangling stories, egos, and conflicting perceptions. But it's also possible for two or more people stuck in a stalemate to call a truce and agree to engage in a collaborative conversation. Much like mediation, such conversations create a dynamic shift in the energy and tone of the conversation. It should be made clear when and by whom a decision will be made. Each participant tells their story without interruption; reveals their facts; and states their feelings, desires, and concerns. In Chapter 7, we will discuss the tools of open advocacy and inquiry, which will enhance the process of creating thoughtful collaborations. We will also explore how invaluable open questions are.

When it comes to open questions, kids are good role models. They are full of questions that demonstrate their curiosity. "Why is the moon orange tonight?" "Why do I need to go to bed now?" "Where does hamburger come from?" "Why isn't Daddy home tonight?" "Why does it hurt when the kids at school tease me?" Socialized and indoctrinated into our communities' norms, we lose some of that innocent curiosity. In school we get gold stars for raising our hands with the answer. In business we get raises, promotions, and bonuses for being the smartest person in the room. I can count on two hands the business meetings I have witnessed where participants were explicitly encouraged to ask probing questions, test assumptions, or suggest a new standard for consideration.

Purposeful collaborative conversations don't diminish the value of expertise or the need to be prepared and informed. Consider the energy that an expert who is expected to have all the answers brings to a conversation. Compare that to the energy of a humble, curious person who values diversity of thought and good questions. Saying, "I don't know," isn't a sign of weakness or vulnerability. It's a demonstration of humility and strength of character. In school and in business, gifted teachers or great leaders know that a combination of honoring expertise, questions, and curiosity creates a safe space and fuels dynamic creative conversations.

Processing our inner thoughts is a good starting point for improving our collaboration skills so they will no longer hijack our emotions or conversations in real-time.

Let's revisit Antonio's left-hand column exercise:

WHAT YOU WERE THINKING AND FEELING	WHAT YOU AND THE OTHER PERSON SAID
Antonio: *Oh boy, here we go again! Jane's continuing saga.*	Jane: "Can you please help out with Mom next week?
Antonio: *She's so clueless about how impossible it is for me to take a week off to help. She has all the time in the world.*	Antonio: "I don't know if I can make it next week to take care of Mom for all three days."
Antonio: *I can't believe you expect me to jeopardize my new project by taking care of Mom for a whole week!*	Jane: "I know that you're super busy, but I think Mom needs to have someone here."
Antonio: *You have no idea how damn busy I am! You have so much free time on your hands. Your kids are in school all day, and you don't work. You have too much time to stupidly obsess over Mom.*	Antonio: "Are the kids in school next week? Can you do it? That would work better for my schedule. Maybe I can do it for one day."
Antonio: *Oh, yeah. Here you go. Hiring help and spending what little money Mom has.*	Jane: "I'll think of something. Maybe I should start advertising for help."
Antonio: *You're not seeing this situation clearly. You're stressing like this is an emergency.*	Antonio: "You know, I'm still not convinced that Mom needs someone full time."
Antonio: *If you'd stop being a control freak, we could figure this out.*	Jane: "Let's talk again soon. Right now I have to take her shopping."

Here's the work Antonio and I did to process his private conversation:

○ *Oh boy, here we go again! Jane's continuing saga.*
(Authority) I asked Antonio what he felt when he wrote this down. He said he was embarrassed by his dismissal of Jane and his mom. This plays out as a power play by Antonio. When I asked him about it, he recognized that he had brushed Jane off and underappreciated all Jane was doing.

○ *She's so clueless about how impossible it is for me to take a week off to help. She has all the time in the world.*

○ *I can't believe you expect me to jeopardize my new project by taking care of Mom for a whole week!*
(Standards) When he reflected on these thoughts, he saw how much he undervalues Jane's work as a mom and home keeper. His ego went full blast, elevating his work and becoming indignant when Jane didn't understand.

○ *You have no idea how damn busy I am! You have so much free time on your hands. Your kids are in school all day, and you don't work. You have too much time to stupidly obsess over Mom.*
(Standards, Concerns) This one struck Antonio hard. He realized it was totally unfair to say that Jane had a stupid obsession over their mom. She was doing a great job taking care of her. He was concerned about how to balance his work and family life, and he began to wonder how he could share the burden.

○ *Oh, yeah. Here you go. Hiring help and spending what little money Mom has. If you'd stop being a control freak, we could figure this out.*
(Concerns) Here Antonio understands how many assumptions he's making because he's afraid of the future. He was worried that he would have to pony up if their mom got worse and ran out of money.

○ *If you'd stop being a control freak, we could figure this out.*
(Desires, Goals) Rather than talking about money, future possibilities, help, and their mom's best interests, he pushed Jane
away and accused her of freaking out. He and Jane never talked
about what they both wanted for their mom and how they could
manage the future as her health declined.

By investigating his private conversations, he uncovered authority
issues, standards through which he valued his work more than Jane's,
concerns about money, and his failure to talk about their mom's future.
Those insights were enough to help him process, rethink, and redesign
his next conversation with Jane.

The next chapter focuses on our patterns of telling and selling our
stories, asking questions, and listening, tools that are key to understanding and transforming how we talk, listen, interact.

PRACTICES

o After completing a left-hand column exercise, read it out loud. Note what feelings and emotions arise. Be kind to yourself.

o Gently process the emotionally charged thoughts and feelings, using facts, emotions, and the four questions.

o Without judgment, own the emotions and search for the story beneath them.

o Can you find ideas that are good, useful, and helpful embedded in the negative talk?

o Revisit the conversation and reflect on how you could redesign it.

o Practice saying the new words out loud. For example: "Jane, I can't help you for three days next week, and I appreciate all you're doing for Mom. Let's take time to talk about what we each want for Mom going forward."

o Note how your ability to transform your ugly private conversations into useful words in the moment improves over time.

OPEN ADVOCACY AND INQUIRY

*The most erroneous stories are those we think we know
best—and therefore never scrutinize or question.*

—STEPHEN JAY GOULD, American evolutionary biologist
and historian of science

n this chapter, we explore patterns of how we tell our stories (advocacy), how we ask questions to understand others' stories (inquiry), and how we listen. We will explore these tools:

○ Open advocacy—the art of stating our perspectives thoughtfully, with humility, curiosity, and confidence

○ Open inquiry—the art of respectfully and nonjudgmentally inquiring into others' perspectives

○ Listening—being present with curiosity, empathy, and an ability to absorb others' stories

We know that clinging to our stories can get us in trouble. When our uninvestigated opinions show up in our interactions, the consequences aren't great. With our ego holding on for dear life, we make our case on autopilot and defensively state our position, or we ask accusatory questions while surreptitiously attempting to prove our point. We don't have to look too far in our daily lives to observe defensive advocacy and inquiry. The frustrated leader blames his staff for their embarrassment in front of his boss. The livid neighbor threatens to call the cops if you don't shut up your dog. Or the team makes excuses for their missed deadline because someone didn't give them the resources they needed to get the job done. In every case, the attachment to a story is the problem. Defensive advocacy and inquiry are closed-minded. In conversation, we hear things like this: "We've done our work. It's the finance team that's holding us up." Or, "We'll be in trouble if we adopt this change." Or, "I've stated my position. You can disagree, but my decision is made." Defensive inquiry is the opposite side of the coin of defensive advocacy. People are also hooked on their story and afraid, and they ask questions that support their story. In conversation, we hear things like this: "How does your position make sense?" Or, "What were you thinking when you signed that agreement?" Or, "Can you give me one example that supports your harsh feedback?"

Antonio and Jane's conversation about their mother was an example of defensive advocacy and inquiry because they were telling their stories and making polite points rather than sincerely asking fair questions of each other. There was little to no inquiry or skillful listening. Neither was consciously aware of their underlying desires, concerns, and standards, and they weren't interested in what the other thought or felt. Both tried in vain to win the argument and convince the other of their position, and their questions lacked honest curiosity. Antonio's question about Jane's schedule was driven by his veiled belief that his work was more important than hers and that she had the free time to take care of their mother. And Jane's initial request was full of prejudgments about Antonio's unwillingness to put the time in to care for their mother.

When we engage in conversations that matter or where the stakes are high, we are usually attached to our position and running on auto-pilot, and we are likely to spin down the spiral. As we hold on, we attack the other's position, strengthening their attachment to that position. We now have two or more people spinning away, defending their unprocessed positions—colliding spirals. Autopilot defensive cycles make collaborative dialogue impossible.

The following is another example of the consequences of failed collaborative conversation.

○ ○

Robert, a top executive at a major music label in New York City, was on a Zoom call with the lawyer, Gina, and the manager, Allen, of a new musician, Samad, recently signed by the label. They had scheduled the meeting to review a strategy for the upcoming year. Robert and Gina had years of experience in the music industry, but Allen and his client were new and excited to be in the game. The contract was a multimillion-dollar deal, and the heat was on to get the ball rolling and produce some big hits.

Robert drew up a plan, which included studio time for recording new music, streaming content, radio play, and podcast interviews. Allen hoped to book bigger performance venues and was skeptical of Robert's plan. Gina knew the contract details and wanted to ensure that the label held up their end of the bargain. Music industry contacts are complex, but doubts and questions were beginning to surface early in the deal. How would the schedules be coordinated? Who made the final call on how to prioritize Samad's time? How much creative independence did Samad have? There are plenty of examples of music artists being locked into contracts with labels that don't live up to their big promises. Gina knew the pitfalls of breaking in a new artist, and she wanted to keep the lines of communication open.

The Zoom call didn't go well. Allen was intimidated by Robert's position, experience, and assertiveness. Insecure, he figured he had to play hardball. He made a few demands about Samad's schedule and his creative control over his music. Gina had seen this all before, and Allen's demands made her impatient and nervous. She tried to slow down the conversation to get agreement on a few simple things—a coordinated timeline and the number of songs to be produced in the next few months. Allen gave no ground and said he would need to talk to Samad. Robert had little patience for Allen's inexperience and ridiculous demands. He just wanted to sign the damn contract so he and his team could put their plan into effect. The meeting ended abruptly, with no resolution and with a hardening of positions.

Defensive Advocacy

Defensive advocacy is contentious (see Figure 6). I think of it as close-fisted storytelling. Indira Gandhi, a former prime minister of India, said, "India wants to avoid a war at all costs, but it is not a one-sided affair. You cannot shake hands with a clenched fist." At this very moment, Russia and its authoritarian leader, Vladimir Putin, are waging war on Ukraine. All diplomatic efforts were a one-sided affair. The West had a weak hand to play against a dictator whose mind was made up and who has a penchant for spouting his version of the truth. At the same time, the US Congress often seems to disintegrate as one side tries to govern and make laws while the other side is hellbent on stopping any progress.

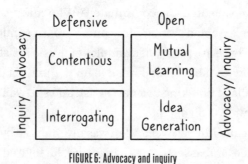

FIGURE 6: Advocacy and inquiry

Why is defensive advocacy so prevalent? As we mentioned in Chapter 6, beginning with our first days in the classroom, the unspoken rule was that we should raise our hands when we had the answer. As young adults, we were admitted into college because we worked hard to have the answers, as demonstrated by our grades and test scores. For decades, we memorized the scripted answers to prove that we are worthy. In much the same way, in the business world we are rewarded for finding the solution to any given problem and being the smartest person in the room. Knowing answers is valued more than asking questions, and that addiction is the root of our inability to collaborate when the stakes are high.

For the most part, close-fisted advocacy is seeking a win-lose outcome. *I'm here to prove my point and win by proving you wrong.* As "knowers," we sound arrogant as we tell our stories—be they fact or fiction—to gain power, prove our authority, and win arguments.

Competition has its place in society. Some domains like sports and education promote challenges by setting high-bar goals and pushing our physical and cognitive potential through rigorous training. In law, a good defense is critical to determining innocence or guilt. But in many domains of life—leadership, team building, politics, community building, social engagements, and family—collaborative conversations serve us well.

In the conversation described earlier, Allen's inexperience and tough-guy stance and Robert's arrogance and inability to work with Allen to find common ground or to share facts about the industry's challenges made collaboration and compromise impossible.

Defensive Inquiry

Defensive inquiry is defensive advocacy's partner in crime, and they are both equally unproductive. Attached to our stories and convinced that we are right, we ask questions that are advocacy masked as inquiry. Our loaded questions feel like an interrogation (see Figure 6). We use it to ask questions to disprove other perspectives. We use it to pull power plays by making it unsafe for others to speak up. And we use it to hide our ignorance when we don't have a clear position. These inquisitions disguised as inquiry play out in hierarchies regularly. Listening be damned—my story will prevail!

Like defensive advocacy, defensive inquiry doesn't serve most conversations. Insincere and self-serving, it shuts out voices and shuts down dialogue.

In the conversation between Antonio and Jane, his questions were masking his belief that Jane had far more free time on her hands than he did. Likewise, Jane's questions about helping their mother disguised her lack of faith in Antonio's commitment to their mother. There was little or no curiosity, and neither listened to the other person's position.

Mindful Listening

There's no shortage of self-help books offering advice on listening, suggesting that we make eye contact, repeat what others say, and mirror their body language. We have all experienced conversations with our inner dialogue running on autopilot. For the most part, our private conversations—working in tandem with the ego—encourage us to cling to and defend our positions with a closed fist. While on defense, we simply can't absorb what other people are saying. Consequently, our ability to listen is greatly diminished. Knowing how multiple stories—spoken and unspoken—can easily collide, we can turn down the volume of our inner voices and create bandwidth to pay attention and mindfully listen.

In conversation, our attention is focused on our feelings, stories, and opinions. Our inner voices, stressed bodies, and cognition take up a ton of energy in frustrating conversations. It takes conscious effort to think on our feet, process our thinking, and formulate our responses. This effort can feel overwhelming, but we can learn to shift a percentage of our self-focused attention externally to others across the table to become better observers and listeners. In challenging conversations, we can become more aware of others' words, feelings, and reactions rather than getting lost in our thoughts and feelings. Beyond listening to their words, we can observe their body language to determine what signals they are sending. We can tune in to the tone of voices. *Is he being defensive? Is she interested in my position?* And we can make eye contact. *Is he looking distracted or worried?* There's lots to discover.

Shifting our attention makes us more present in the moment and changes how others perceive us. As we mindfully listen to others, we are more accessible to them, and they can feel the focus of our attention. It's a win-win for conversations, and our presence signals to others that we are open and want to hear and understand. When we are present, we can be better informed so we can read the energy of the people in the room, which can help us navigate the conversation.

I have three older sisters and a younger brother. My youngest sister is a lovely, talented, and beautiful woman, but she carries a life-long burden of suffering because she was abused as a young woman. I won't share the details of her unconscionable experiences, but her story helped me learn about listening, asking questions, and accepting others' struggles and sorrow. Most of the details are fuzzy in my head, but I know that when my sister told her story, it took years for other family members and me to absorb and accept her truth fully. Looking back, I realize that I wrestled with my denial for way too long. Accepting—but not always liking or loving—reality is crucial for how we listen to and love others. Open hearts and minds shape our relationships and affect our wellbeing.

Miscommunications, misunderstandings, and conflicts disrupt our daily patterns. When a comment or criticism catches us off guard, we react on autopilot, and we feel upset, angry, or in disbelief. These disruptions can also be a wake-up call, and a break in a pattern can be a signal to investigate that pattern. We can learn something about ourselves and our stories in those moments. Mindful listening is difficult, but when done well, it's a gift for both the listener and the speaker. It's also a prerequisite for practicing open advocacy and inquiry.

Open Advocacy and Inquiry

Open-Handed Advocacy and Inquiry =
Mutual Learning = Idea Generation

Open advocacy and inquiry resolve problems by encouraging transparency and mutual learning (see Figure 6). We release our stories from a clenched fist with open advocacy, acknowledging that our story is one of many and becoming comfortable with the idea of not having the "right" answer. When we have the intention of learning, we are free to unclench our fists to reveal our thinking with an open hand. The four questions are our guide for not only processing our inner dialogue and finding the golden nuggets within them but also for learning to reveal our desires, concerns, and standards.

With open inquiry, we ask sincere questions about others' desires, concerns, and standards. The four questions are an excellent tool for shaping our sincere questions, which open up space in any conversation by creating safety. When I ask teams the four questions, the unspoken gradually finds its way to the surface.

In all conversations, it's helpful to be mindful of what we can control and what we can't. Bryon Katie, a spiritual teacher, reminds us that there are three kinds of business: our business, others' business, and God's business. When we are emotionally triggered, it's good to ground ourselves by asking ourselves whose business we are in. What authority do we have to be in God's or other people's business? We do have authority to be in our own business. We can work with our emotions and stories to change our thinking and behavior. If we are judging others' feelings, perspectives, or decisions, and we desperately want them to change, we are in their business. Even knowing that futility, it's challenging to break the pattern. And when we are upset and can't accept the truth of what is happening right in front of our nose, we are in God's business. When we point a finger judging others, there are always four pointing back to us.

In both earlier examples—Jane and Antonio, Robert and Allen— their public conversations were more or less civilized, but issues of power quietly orchestrated their interactions with little or no give and take, exacerbating the problems in their relationship. They shared words, but they couldn't honestly communicate their thoughts and feelings. Stymied, they couldn't compromise or find reasonable solutions. They simply didn't know how to productively advocate and persuade, to find common ground, to ask nonjudgmental questions, or to explore new ideas about how to solve their differences.

Had Robert changed his attitude about Allen's inexperience by understanding how challenging it is for a young manager to navigate the complex world of major record labels, he could have easily shifted the conversation. Persuasive advocacy and a few questions about Allen's concerns and goals could have settled Allen's insecurities, allowing them to reach a compromise.

When Antonio processed his private conversation with Jane, he discovered that he was so singularly focused on his project that he hadn't given much thought to his mother's care. He also uncovered his concerns, and he became aware that he considered his time far more valuable than Jane's. Those insights were enough to help him unwind from his unexplored stories and to ask open, honest questions that helped him understand Jane, all of which allowed him to work with her.

Open-handed advocacy and inquiry are addictive. When one person shows a bit of vulnerability, others drop their guard because vulnerability begets vulnerability. Open-handed conversations are far more persuasive than close-fisted arguments. As my wife reminds me, "You catch more flies with honey than with vinegar." Letting down our defenses, we can rekindle a sense of humor and enjoy a healthy give and take. Less stress, less judgment, more learning, more connection, and more ease— what's not to love about that? Conversations are lighter, provocative, and constructive when we become more adept at balancing advocacy and inquiry.

Balancing Advocacy and Inquiry

Practicing open advocacy and inquiry doesn't mean we give up our positions or roll over in silence. It means that we assert our perspective productively and openly, ask sincere questions, and invite others to meet join in.

There's no perfect recipe for balancing advocacy and inquiry. The best we can do is to be present, observe, listen, and assess our next best move. That might be more advocacy, more questions, or more silence. If we are confused because what someone is saying differs from their body language, we ask a few good questions. Or if we don't think what we said is registering, we can try to advocate our position in a new way. Collaborative conversations are a dance. If I'm in 4/4 time (1,2,3,4; 1,2,3,4) and the other person is doing the waltz (1,2,3; 1,2,3), it's time to change our approach. A balance of open advocacy and inquiry combines persuasive and receptive qualities.

It's important to note that even when we are doing our best, we will meet resistance. People can be mean spirited, immature, insecure, or ignorant. They argue, interrupt, doubt, or lie because they are stuck and fearful because their egos are at stake. In the face of this kind of resistance, our best move is to make our case briefly and use inquiry to test their willingness to engage. If they won't explore facts or reveal their reasoning, or they show no interest in understanding our position, our best move is to bow out graciously.

In hierarchical conversations, power issues make finding a balance tricky. "My one-on-ones with my boss are frustrating. I'm never sure where he stands, and I'm afraid to second guess him." Or, "In my meetings with the executive committee, I never get through my slides. A few leaders take the floor and rant about this or that, and we never get to have a productive conversation." In both circumstances, authority is the elephant in the room, leaving conversation close fisted rather than open handed.

A common mistake and imbalance between advocacy and inquiry is over-advocating. When we are so sure of a position, we want to present as much information as possible. We can over explain or kill a meeting with tedious, endless slides. The meeting is bloated with too much information and there is no absorbable message or productive dialogue.

These meetings end with issues unresolved and participants wondering why they just wasted two hours.

In architecture, a *parti* is a principle for organizing the complexities of a building program. It's a single diagram or sketch that encompasses many diverse elements. This concept is a different way to advocate. I introduce my clients to the parti tool as an example of how to get our heads out of the weeds and into the clouds. Engineering, sciences, and education are all complex systems that can be overwhelming. When advocating, I see the tendency for many to dive into details of whatever problem issues is at hand. This would be like planning a house and worrying over the style of door or kitchen cabinets without having a broad concept of the style, mass, and proportions. In persuading others it is far better to start at a high level and bring others along on a journey. A good practice is to purposefully strike a balance between information shared and discussions. Instead of the arduous work of trying to convince with information overload, we can create presentations that tell a story in smaller bits and pieces with simple and direct slides that encourage dialogue. Or we can start a presentation with high-level slides of the key elements and discuss how they interrelate. In both cases, this is advocacy in brief. We drop a bit of well-organized information and paint a picture for easy comprehension. Then we shift the dance to inquiry. "Does this agenda make sense to you?" Or, "Given the overall picture, is there a particular set of issues you'd like to focus on?" A balanced process is more likely to elicit curious reactions from the boss, team, and audience inviting them to share how or what they're thinking.

Our best shot at balancing advocacy and inquiry is to be present and pay attention to others in the room. It's a dance that requires some experimenting and practice. Here are a few ways to begin:

○ Take a breath and notice your feelings.

○ Ground yourself in your seat. Feel your feet on the floor. Take note of your posture.

- Be aware of power imbalances between the people in the conversation.

- Respect the authority of others and use your power well.

- Depending on the circumstances (power, energy, body language, etc.), assess whether you should begin with open advocacy or inquiry.

- Start with advocacy in brief, a high-level view to orient your audience.

- If uncertain, begin with inquiry.

- Give your full attention. Ask a question using one of the four questions and be sincere about wanting to understand their position. "Do we agree on what our goal is for this meeting?"

- Depending on their response, you can ask another question for clarity. Something like this: "Let me make sure I understand. You're worried about X, right?"

- Look for common ground—facts, concerns, shared goals—to create mutual learning and to build bridges between your thinking.

- You might then switch and advocate your position, noting a contrast or an interesting difference. That could sound something like this: "I was measuring our success by X, but it sounds like you're thinking about it differently. For me, that's a new way to think about it. Let's walk through it."

- Stay open, be curious, and be a good observer.

- Create safe space by making it safe for others to ask you questions.

Here's the conversation Antonio hoped to have after he processed his private conversation:

Jane: "Can you please help out with Mom next week?"

Antonio: "I'm glad you're asking for help. You're doing a lot for Mom, and I haven't been available."

Jane: "I know that you're super busy, but I think Mom needs to have someone here."

Antonio: "My schedule is nuts, and I'm sure you have your hands full with the kids and Bob. What days next week are the toughest for you? I'll try to squeeze in some half days. And while I'm there, let's talk about what Mom needs going forward."

Jane: "That would be great. Let me look at my week. Honestly, I'm not sure what to do. I could use your smarts to put a plan together."

Antonio: "Maybe there are some solutions out there that we don't know about. Let's talk about that."

Jane: "Thanks. I'm about to take Mom shopping, so I'll get back to you about next week."

The work Antonio did to process his private conversation paid off. He was looking forward to his next conversation with Jane. It might not go precisely as he had planned, but he was leaving his old patterns behind.

Like Antonio, we can free ourselves of old, harmful patterns of judgment and become more effective collaborators. In relationships, we can build rapport and mutual respect. And the way we coordinate action with others can be more seamless, rewarding, and successful.

Good collaborative conversations prepare us for creative conversations because open minds and open hearts are a prerequisite for creativity.

PRACTICES

o Put on your observation hat in a meeting. Note how people are advocating and pushing their opinion. Note the quality of the questions. Are they open and curious, or are they disguised advocacy?

o Note your patterns of advocacy and inquiry. When are you in defensive mode? When do you push your agenda or ask leading questions? Think about where your patterns might have originated. Who were your role models?

o Observe your listening patterns. When are you rehearsing your rebuttal in your head? When are you making a sincere effort to understand others' perspectives? Practice setting aside your assumptions and your positions to make space in your mind to be influenced or changed.

o Practice open advocacy by revealing details of your thinking. Process your negative judgments, then turn them into helpful ideas that you can share. Reveal your desires and check for common goals. Check for power issues. Build bridges by sharing your concerns and standards and listening for agreement.

o Practice open inquiry to understand where others are coming from. After sharing your desires and concerns with care and curiosity, ask about theirs. Can your questions help them be more reflective or revealing?

o Invite others into collaborative conversations. In meetings or discussions, model the skills of open advocacy and inquiry, and encourage all to take time to work through disagreements with a win-win attitude.

Part III

CREATIVE CONVERSATIONS
Trust Your Intuition

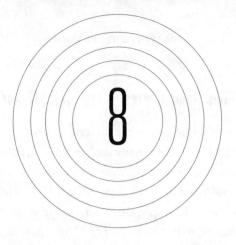

8

FROM RESIGNATION TO WONDER

I believe in intuition and inspiration... Imagination is more important than knowledge. For knowledge is limited, whereas imagination embraces the entire world, stimulating progress, giving birth to evolution. It is, strictly speaking, a real factor in scientific research.

—ALBERT EINSTEIN

As we observe, detangle, and disidentify with any story (ours or those of others), we reap the benefits of a wider lens. We become a source of curiosity and wonder, at the top of the funnel, where we access possibilities and creativity.

In this chapter, we explore the right and left hemispheres of our brain, how they influence our lives. We take a look at resignation compared to wonder, the value of intuition and presence, and the art of co-creating with others.

The Two Hemispheres of the Brain: IQ and EQ

Our brains have two distinct hemispheres, joined together by a busy, super neural connector called the corpus callosum. Successful creative conversations require us to pay respect and attention to the underappreciated right brain and to sync it up with our logical left brain.

Historically, the left hemisphere, which Einstein called a faithful servant, was believed to be the seat of our logic, helping us think rationally about details, sequencing, concreteness, and analysis. It allows us to agree on facts and compare this versus that. It's the glue of our communities, our institutions, and society.

The right side, embraced by Einstein as a sacred gift, is about context, emotion, the big picture, and unification. It helps us interpret incoming signals, understand different ideas simultaneously, read emotions and nonverbal cues, and access our intuition.

After years of misunderstanding, neuroscience research has dispelled misconceptions about the independence of the two hemispheres, allowing us to see what's happening inside the black box of our head. It's fascinating to know that the two hemispheres seamlessly work together and complement one another in crucial ways. In fact, Iain McGilchrist, the grandfather of neuroscientific research, has confirmed Einstein's intuitions, declaring the right hemisphere the master and the left hemisphere its messenger. His book, *The Master and His Emissary: The Divided Brain and the Making of the Western World,* sheds light on the ways that they integrate and synthesize to provide us with a singular interpretation of the world, defining us as the thinkers and actors we are.

Western societies have historically favored the left hemisphere. Much like the Industrial Age, the Information Age rewards and values logic and IQ. As a culture, our values evolved to lionize the left hemisphere. For most of the twentieth century, intelligence quotient (IQ) has been the prime measure of human intelligence. Only in the last twenty years have researchers explored emotional quotient (EQ) as a measure of intelligence. EQ is the measure of an individual's ability to recognize, discern, and manage emotions. In its short history, the study of EQ has dramatically increased our understanding of human feelings and their connection to our thoughts and interactions, and EQ is no longer a shadow of IQ. Researchers now consider EQ an equal—if not the leading—partner in the understanding of human dynamics.

So, what does this mean for our ability to have creative conversations? The storytelling and collaborative conversations are right-brain activities that enhance our EQ, our tolerance, our empathy, and our compassion, preparing us to reconsider our patterns related to creativity.

Generally speaking, we have innate preferences and patterns that favor our left or right brain. Those with a natural inclination or learned behavior for left-brain thinking may have to work harder at relationships and creative endeavors. They might be attracted to logically oriented careers like law, the trades, engineering, or accounting. Those with right-brain preferences or learned behavior might struggle to get their taxes done or might have a hard time settling down to do their nitty-gritty paperwork. They might be caregivers, artists, entrepreneurs, or musicians. These are generalizations, but they are helpful for observing and understanding how our preferences play out in conversations.

For example, in designing a new building, my natural inclination is to be curious about concepts, design, and the environmental context of the project (a weighted right-hemisphere activity). I would begin the process thinking big, generating a parti—a broad conceptual idea. Others would naturally gravitate to zoning issues, site attributes, budgets, and programming requirements (a weighted left-hemisphere activity). They were collecting data and understanding constraints and the building context from a different vantage point than I was.

Whether our preference is conceptual or data driven, neither is "right." Defending our preference is noncollaborative, and it limits our creativity. Like the integration of the two hemispheres, the conceptual and the specific are complementary. Left brainers should have no fear that the world will lose respect for the IQ. The left brain will serve us well and bring a crazy right-brain idea back to Earth. We can dream, create, and imagine possibilities until the cows come home, but we do our best work when those ideas meet our rational mind, where we can weigh the options, make a good decision, and get the job done. The collaboration of the two hemispheres of the brain is a model for framing differences as complementary and productive rather than competitive and nonproductive.

The technical revolution and the evolution of human consciousness are slowly and gradually recognizing the value that our right brain brings to the table. In his book *A Whole New Mind: Why Right-Brainers Will Rule the Future*, Daniel Pink talks about the coming "Conceptual Age," a time when the economy will rely more on occupations that demand right-brain talent. Thanks to the rise of AI, many analytic and repetitive left-minded jobs (e.g., finance, medicine, engineering, and law) will be more efficiently done by faster and faster computers. But AI can't create authenticity, art, originality, or hands-on work. During the Conceptual Age, societies will value influencers, teachers, builders, artists, inventors, and leaders who creatively inspire us to navigate a technologically oriented future.

Resignation vs. Acceptance of Possibilities

Creative conversations are the force that lifts us up and propels us toward new ways of thinking and new ideas. It's the opposing force of thinking patterns that defend our old stories and keep us in our comfort zones. When unexpected life events fly in the face of our hopes and dreams, challenging our precious stories, we can rest in comfort, or we can accept the invitation to stretch into unknown possibilities. Unfortunately, our egos don't quietly march into the night, effortlessly accepting change.

In Chapter 2, I presented the spiral diagram, which shows how the nonacceptance of reality spins us down, causing resentment to build. *These things shouldn't happen. Life isn't fair. This can't be!* In this chapter, we explore how our inability to accept possibilities or to imagine a new future can spin us down, culminating in a pattern of resignation. *I'll never get out of this mess. There's no way this relationship will end well. I hate my boss, but I'm stuck with this damn job.*

These patterns of resentment and resignation are related because both arise from nonacceptance. In our investigation of facts, we discovered how the acceptance of facts moves us up the spiral out of resentment helping us come to peace with reality. In creative conversations, we are uplifted from the drag of resignation by accepting possibilities to discover a world of wonder and unexplored futures (see Figure 7).

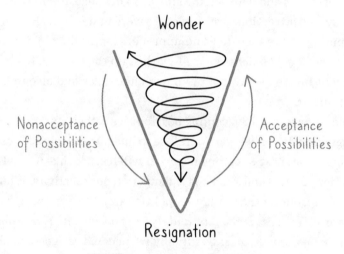

Wonder

Nonacceptance
of Possibilities

Acceptance
of Possibilities

Resignation

FIGURE 7: The spiral of wonder vs. resignation

I didn't go to college right out of high school (long story) and in 1969 I was snared in the Vietnam war draft. I enrolled in the National Guard (another story for another time) to avoid being drafted. At the time, I was a professional musician and working at an architectural firm as a copy boy. Over four years, as my interests in design, architectural history, and theory grew, I was struck by the architecture bug. With the encouragement of a friend and colleague, Rick Reeder, I decided to satisfy the bug and a get a degree in architecture. My academic credentials were not great, so it was a gift to discover the unique Boston Architectural College. It was the only accredited work/study architectural degree in the country. It had an open admissions process (easy to get into and tough to complete), and it was very reasonably priced—all essential given my circumstances.

When I shared my dream with my buddies at the firm before moving to Boston, they were very supportive. But my other friends laughed at me, doubting my dream and my ability to pull it off. "You, an architect?! That's crazy! Moving to a big city with your wife, dog, and no job is super risky. You'll get eaten alive." I could have bought into the doubts of others and believed the stories in my head, but my intuition, curiosity, and attraction to architecture were undeniable. Rather than succumbing to the disbelief and apprehension, I had a clear revelation: *If I don't go, I'll never know!* I worked up the courage to embrace a different future, one full of unknown challenges and also unknown opportunities.

This was a lesson in accepting possibilities rather than succumbing to resignation. When we can't or refuse to imagine or embrace possibilities, tomorrow, next week, and next year will feel a lot like today. Limiting stories—fearful and stuck—is a damper on our creativity. When our job, our boss, our mother-in-law, or politics aren't to our liking, we spin downward. *This boss is the pits, and there's no way out! That woman is going to ruin my marriage!* Eventually we become resigned, unable to imagine a different future.

As I mentioned in Chapter 3, writing down our strong judgments and asking the four questions helps us observe and clarify our thinking. If we don't write them down, our thoughts and feelings are a confusing mush in our heads. For the creative conversations, writing our doubts and fears helps us to catch ourselves as we slide down into resignation. With less judgment, we can slow down, adopt an "I don't know," or "I wonder if" frame of mind. We can let the creative juices flow, exhilarated by what could be. It shouldn't be surprising to discover how difficult this can be, given how frequently we are rewarded for having the answer at home, school, and work. The four questions guide the way. We can ask a few key questions to create space in our mind so slivers of light can penetrate our thinking. *Are my desires or worries blinding me to a different future? Are my self-doubts robbing me of what I'm capable of? Are my standards/judgments limiting my ability to envision an outside-the-box opportunity?*

○ ○

Melany has been a director in the corporate communications team for three months and she is spiraling into resignation. Frustrated with her boss, Erik, an executive VP, she tells herself, *Erik is the pits. He's mean-spirited and overbearing, and clearly he doesn't respect or compensate women equally. He's well connected and loved upstairs, of course, so no one stands up to him. He has too much damn power. I shouldn't have taken this job. I'm screwed.*

After a few coaching sessions, Melany agrees to write down her thoughts, feelings, and emotions, and the facts, based on the four questions.

Facts

I know that Erik has fired others for speaking up and disagreeing with him. We all know that he's well regarded by the CEO, and they're regular golfing buddies.

We also know for a fact that people have gone to HR about this guy, and HR has said, "There's nothing we can do. It's politically complicated."

Desires

I want appreciation for my team's good work, fair compensation, and opportunities for growth. I wish he'd just shut up sometimes and let us do our work.

Concerns

I don't believe I can speak to anyone about how we're being treated, and there doesn't seem to be anyone who can help us. I could be stuck here forever. I think someone might lose it one day. Maybe me!

Authority

While I accept the company hierarchy, I feel that Erik abuses his power and belittles his employees. Because his abuse and belittling hasn't been addressed, I have to live with his behavior, which is crummy. I recognize that I have no control over my future with the company, and I can't control what's going to happen next.

Standards

I believe that employees should be able to speak their minds. I know that leaders have the responsibility to make decisions, but I believe multiple voices make teams smarter. We should bring our best thinking to our meetings. Leaders with big egos shouldn't be allowed to stomp on their employees with no accountability.

Melany was surprised by the thoughts and feelings that surfaced in her responses. As she wrote them down, she began to recognize her slide toward resignation. She gradually feels less charged as her emotions dissipate and other new ideas surface. When she writes down the facts, her anger pops up: *Ridiculous! How can he and his boss be best friends and run the business the way they do? His overpowering authority shouldn't go unchecked!* She realizes those words are fighting the reality right in front of her: *They're best friends, and I'm not going to change that or how they wield their power.* These are the facts, and her anger and frustrations won't change them. With that realization, she slowly accepts the facts as they are, rather than what she thinks they should be. She also accepts that she has zero control over the situation. She becomes less frustrated, stops spinning, and feels more centered. She has given up her futile fight with reality and now has a better mindset to explore her resignation.

What sticks for her are the desires and standards she wrote down. Her issues with authority began to dissipate once she accepted the reality of the situation. She feels good acknowledging her desire to help her team do good work, and she's very clear about her right to be compensated fairly. As for her standards, she continues to believe they are fair. She would like to work at a place with shared standards. Who doesn't?

As Melany processes her stories, she has a few aha moments. She shifts from feeling resigned to wondering what else might be possible, and eventually she decides to have a conversation with the one HR rep, Carlos, who she believes she can trust.

> Melany: *Carlos, I hope this can be a totally confidential conversation. I've been upset for some time with Erik, but I've been working with Chuck lately, and he has helped me think more clearly about my situation.*

> Carlos: *Of course this is confidential. What's got you so upset?*

> Melany: *I know that Erik is well thought of in the C suites, and I most likely can't influence him or the other leaders, but I think it's important for someone to say that his leadership is overbearing. He's constantly doubting our work, and he doesn't appreciate our successes or our efforts. I'm not sure what's next, but I can't continue to work for someone so misogynistic, and I want to explore my options with you.*

> Carlos: *I get it. Erik's behavior isn't a secret around here, but the CEO isn't willing to address his leadership style directly. Are you interested in exploring other jobs in other departments?*

> Melany: *Maybe. Let me think about it. I have a great team, and I'd hate to leave them stuck with Erik, especially since I have no idea who might replace me.*

> Carlos: *Good point. Let me think about a few possibilities. In the meantime, you should consider having coffee or lunch with a few other leaders. You have a stellar reputation, so don't be shy in seeking out a few leaders to explore lateral move opportunities.*

> Melany: *Thanks for chatting. This has been a rough ride for me, but I'm now far less stressed, and I can think clearly about my options.*

Carlos: *You're very welcome. Let's talk in two weeks and compare notes.*

Melany: *Deal. In the meantime, if you have any other ideas, please reach out to me.*

After this conversation, Melany had new ideas about what's possible for her. She listed the skills she had that could translate to other jobs. She wrote down a list of jobs in other departments and at other companies with good reputations. She jotted down the downsides of staying put (e.g., a culture that doesn't align with her desires and standards). She got excited about dusting off her résumé, making a list of people she could reach out to, and exploring external leadership opportunities.

After Covid hit and work-from-home jobs exploded all across the country, her search broadened. She talked with friends and her significant other about her newfound ideas with a new sense of excitement. She also had a good laugh at her formerly stuck self.

○ ○

Let's look at another example.

In his resignation, John tells himself, *My mother-in-law is going to ruin my marriage! She comes for visits, stays too long, and takes over the whole house. I can't watch the TV shows I want, and she always complains about our meals. This will drive me to drink.*

Hoping to blunt his frustration, he writes out his emotions, some facts, his thoughts, and the four questions (Note: the order of the questions isn't important, but always start with emotions and facts).

Facts

John recognizes that he's hopelessly stuck with his mother-in-law, Mary. He finally decides to chat with his wife, Maureen. She reminds him that Mary is an only child who has been very privileged her whole life. She almost always gets what she wants, and she's a control freak with zero interest in developing self-awareness. After multiple chats, he slowly and reluctantly accepts this fact and realizes that he's not going to change her, but he still doesn't like what's happening. He desperately wants the visits to change (desires). Acceptance isn't rolling over and not caring. Accepting reality can be painful and clarifying, but ultimately it frees us to think about how to solve a problem more creatively.

Desires

He writes down his strong dislike for Mary's behavior. Why can't she be more like his mom, Sue, who is relaxed and easy-going and who knows how long to stay? This is the first time that he recognizes that his dislike for Mary was an unconscious desire that she be more like his mom. In writing these thoughts, John realizes that his hidden desire was at the root of his nonacceptance of his mother-in-law. This desire set up a battle with reality, making him crazy and resentful. But she will never be like his mom. She is who she is.

Concerns

John is concerned that his anger and his inability to deal with Mary has him at odds with his wife. Although he is upset with Mary, the last thing he wants is to allow his mother-in-law to drive a wedge between him and Maureen.

Authority and Standards

John realizes that he's feeling powerless. Exploring his power issues, he sees that he's giving Mary and her bad behavior all the power in this situation. He has an aha moment when he understands that he's allowing Mary's behavior to take over the house and drive him crazy. As he works through his resignation, he wonders what he can change. How can he coexist with Mary without spinning out? Can he and Maureen set new rules (standards) about Mary's visits? How can he not give up his authority around meals and TV?

John asks Maureen to sit down and talk about what he's been think-ing. He tells her about the work he's been doing on his story and how his uninvestigated anger gave Mary the power to upset the household. He asks Maureen if they could set some new rules about Mary's visits. She is relieved to finally talk to John openly. She acknowledges that she too is upset and is beginning to feel resigned to the thought that mother-in-law/son-in-law relationships are doomed. Together they brainstorm ideas about what they could do to change their pattern. John suggests limiting the amount of time of Mary's visits. Maureen suggests that they let Mary know that there are a few hours of TV that are nonnegotiable. They agree to engage with Mary more directly with their concerns in real time and to support one another if things get weird (standards). They make up a signal (both hands on the top of their heads) to alert the other that someone needs to speak up or chill out. The conversation helps both John and Mary feel more aware, lighter, more connected, and more hopeful.

○ ○

Life is a package deal: the good comes with the bad. Regardless of our status, wealth, luck, or misfortune, some things will go our way, but plenty of things will challenge us and our stories. When we accept what life throws our way we are more likely to creatively deal with problems and conflicts we encounter.

PRACTICES

o Pay attention to the left and right sides of your brain during the day. When are you rational, determined, and focused? When do you go with the flow, express yourself creatively, and allow things to unfold? Which feels more natural? They are both useful and complementary ways of being.

o Read a book on emotional intelligence. Daniel Goleman's *Emotional Intelligence* is a good place to start. Notice the areas of life where you're aware of your emotions and you can successfully manage them, and notice the areas where you're emotionally triggered. There are a few easily available online tests if you would like to have a sense of where you fall on the EQ spectrum.

o Note, without judgment, small ways that you slide down toward resignation (no hope, no curiosity)? What circumstances, people, events tend to be triggers?

o Begin to pay attention to the nuances of your feelings so you can be more subtly emotionally attuned. This grows our emotional antennas, increasing our ability to understand and empathize with others and ourselves.

o Read something that is a total stretch, something new that challenges your boundaries, tests your standards, or pushes you to think outside the box.

o Practice shifting gears to adopt a mindset of wonder, "what might be." Allow yourself to imagine possibilities without prejudgment. How do you feel when you make the shift?

o When you don't like what is happening in the moment, note the small ways that you fight reality. Write down, acknowledge, and accept the facts. How does that effect your mindset?

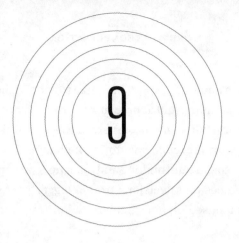

INTUITION AND PRESENCE

*You can't think about presence, and the
mind can't understand it. Understanding
presence is being present.*

—ECKHART TOLLE

love how quantum physics theories can stretch our imaginations and
illustrate the role that awareness and attention play in life. One of the
basic quantum physics theories is that a quantum object can be a wave
and a particle simultaneously. Waves spread out and can be two places at
once, but particles are located in only one place at a time, and they travel
in a single direction. Waves and particles both exist at the same time as
possibilities. Just like when you throw a pebble into a pond, quantum
waves expand and become wider and wider waves of possibilities, until
they collapse into a thought or an object upon observation. How they are
measured and who is looking for what determines what the observer
will see. In other words, the observer's observation determines how so
much of life unfolds.

I'm far from a quantum expert, but I like to use the theories as a metaphor for understanding and appreciating the creative conversation. As individuals, we are particular observers of the world. We see, hear, and experience the world through our stories, beliefs, and patterns of thinking. And as we expand our thinking and open up to new possibilities, we get to make choices and decisions from a bigger pool of possibilities. If we are laser focused on a particular outcome, we are blind to other possibilities.

Neuroscience has only begun to tap into the inner workings of our minds, but at this point, plenty of research supports the hypothesis that holds that self-awareness and mindfulness help a person manifest life.

It's intriguing how these neuroscience concepts are beginning to intersect with ancient wisdom traditions. The practices of prayer, meditation, mindfulness, and yoga all have elements of self-observation, contemplation, thoughtfulness, and introspection. By measuring the different states of mind of long-time meditators, neuroscience has unveiled the physical and psychological benefits of meditation and mindfulness. They include reduced anxiety, improved sleep, increased focus, and a broader sense of wellbeing. In meditation, we pay attention to our inner world: our breath, our physical sensations, and the thoughts swirling about our minds. It's a practice for managing our minds and cultivating our witness.

These practices introduce us to higher states of consciousness, states of mind in which we are open to and accepting of what life throws our way. We can experience flow, a state where we're fully present in the action, a zone where we aren't ruminating on what to do, a space where the body and mind are aligned. Athletes perform miraculous feats in the zone. Artists become conduits for expression from a greater source. Scientists discover theories and resolve quandaries. And in our interactions with others, when we are fully present and open, conversations can flow with a natural, respectful give and take.

There has been plenty written about the power of being present in the moment. *The Power of Now*, a book by Eckhart Tolle, lays out the benefits and the challenges of being present. How can we relax into the moment, trusting life to unfold? Fully present, we focus on the here and now.

Mindful Wandering

Life gets so busy that we rarely take the time to *be* with what is right in front of us. Undistracted and in the moment, we can soak up a beautiful day, the joy of kids playing at the park, the upset in the eyes of a loved one, the unconditional love of our dog. A practice that I have is to go out on my land (two acres—our little piece of heaven) without a plan, open to whatever shows up. Plenty happens. With no conscious effort, I find that things that need attention crop up and I am attracted to them. The weeds need to be pulled. A downed tree can be cut up for next year's firewood. It might be the right time to prune a bush. Or my finicky chainsaw won't start and needs some tinkering. These experiences require a letting go, learning to trust life to unfold minute by minute—a taste of flow.

Similarly, over the years, I've noticed more subtle intuitions. When fully present, I hear quiet whispering, *Did you leave something in the hotel room?* Or, *Time to make the call you've been avoiding.* Or, *Today's the day to finish the tough chapter you've been putting off.* Just last week, a big windstorm came our way. I woke up worried about an oak tree twenty feet from our bedroom window and right next to my new truck. I didn't listen to that intuition, and the next morning, my wife looked out the window and saw the tree lying across my truck. Argh! If only I had listened!

When we listen to our intuitions (often our private thoughts) during stressful interactions, we can discover their golden nuggets. *I'm afraid this decision is going to backfire.* Or, *My gut is telling me to speak up, or this behavior will never stop.* Or, *I really want those new computers for the team, but right now might not be the best time to spend that kind of capital.* Suppressed intuitions—fearful or helpful—are missed opportunities.

The Big Move

Heather, who lives with her family in London, is offered an exciting new executive job with a prominent technology company in Silicon Valley. After heart-wrenching conversations with her husband and two children about schools, cultural changes, friends, and extended family, they collectively agree to move from the UK to the US. That move takes time and requires lots of paperwork, conversations, and adjustments.

After months of settling in with the family and six months of dedicated work, things aren't looking as rosy as Heather had projected. She seems resigned to having made a bad decision.

Heather reports directly to Robert, the CEO. In short order, Heather is incredibly challenged. In meetings, Robert always seems to have the right answers, doesn't listen, and always has to have the last word, often overriding her decisions. Her role changes several times, and with each succeeding change, she has less and less responsibility. After all the effort it took to move her family, she's angry that the CEO is a jerk and that she can't lead her team. Heather isn't feeling it. An inner voice is telling her to escape the madness, but her fears about change are even louder.

When Heather and I worked together, I was curious about her intuitions, so I asked her to explore the four questions and to acknowledge her intuitions.

Heather's Four Questions:

○ What are my desires?

- ○ What I want most is a stable job that aligns with my values and challenges me intellectually. My intuitions are telling me to make a break and move on.

- ○ My fears about changing jobs keeps me from imagining other possibilities. I can't imagine a different future.

○ What are my concerns?

- ○ My primary concern is for the future of my family.

- ○ I feel guilty about uprooting the family and worry about yet another change.

- ○ I am concerned that changing jobs will look bad on my résumé.

○ Which of my standards are driving my opinions?

  ○ There's a large gap between my standards of excellence and my boss's standards.

  ○ My standards of great leadership center around holding people to high standards and solving problems creatively and coaching them to do their best.

  ○ My new boss's blame and shame are opposite of what I expected.

  ○ My intuition tells me that my standards would never be met at this organization.

○ What issues of authority or power play out in this situation?

  ○ I unconsciously let my boss's behavior drive my feelings. At times I want to give him a piece of my mind.

  ○ I acknowledge that my boss intimidates me and that I fear losing my job. My intuition tells me to talk this over with my family to help decide my best move.

By investigating her thoughts and intuitions via the four questions, Heather became more positive and hopeful. Her fears were displaced by a voice that told her that she could satisfy her desires and keep her standards, and the family would be all for it. She went from feeling stuck and resigned to taking walks to ponder her future by herself and with her husband. He reminded her that her talents and work were in high demand and that moving around is the norm for people in Silicon Valley. When Heather accepted the reality of the situation, her mood shifted. She decided to have a conversation with a trusted colleague and a top recruiter. As she began imagining new possibilities, opportunities started to show up. Within two months, Heather landed a promotion and a better job at a successful startup with a proven leadership team.

○ ○

One of the hardest lessons to learn in creative conversations is letting go of control. We are well programmed to do, do, do, convinced that if we try hard enough, we can control everything coming our way. Wayne Liquorman, one of my teachers, teaches a metaphor that has stuck with me. Do you remember as a kid at a carnival being on a ride where you were driving a fire engine, hot rod car, or train? Watching the kids is delightful and fun and it stirs up old memories of our experiences. The kids are having a blast steering the fire truck. But as we know, their steering wheel isn't connected to anything. It was and is an illusion.

Wayne's point is similar to Byron Katie's question on whose business we are in. They invite us to be realistic about what we can and can't control. *What's has happened in my life that was not on my radar screen? What is happening due to the complexities and intricacies of life of which I have no power? How are my expectations at odds with what happens?*

As I began to practice, paying attention to the gap between my expectations and the reality of life, I noticed that my illusory steering wheel isn't as connected as I thought. Life sometimes aligns with my desires, but it's equally true that life often takes an unexpected turn. We can fight and maintain our quest for control, or we can accept life as it comes, be fully present, and go with the flow.

John Lennon famously said, "Life is what happens when we are busy making other plans." That can be a hard pill to swallow for many people. When we think we have our future all figured out, life delivers a blow to our best laid plans. All of life is a complex connected mystery of synergistic events unfolding in incomprehensible ways. The metaphor of the steering wheel is a reminder to be more aware of how we battle facts and reality in our daily lives. As the Serenity Prayer says, "God grant me the serenity to accept the things I cannot change, courage to change the things I can, and wisdom to know the difference."

There will be easy days when our desires line up with reality and challenging days when it's a struggle to accept what we don't like. On the good days, we can be present in the moment, we can stay cool when things shift against our wishes, and we can bear witness to our thoughts with curiosity about what's possible.

The creativity conversation asks each of us to explore the patterns and distractions that keep us fighting with reality. We build on our work with stories by improving our ability to engage in open advocacy and inquiry in order to become more present in the moment and more open to new possibilities.

PRACTICES

o Experiment with meditation, prayer, and yoga and note
   how they can help you increase your ability to be more
   present and mindful in real time.

o Experiment with unplanned activities. Start gardening,
   cleaning, cooking, dancing, writing, drawing, playing
   music, and so on. Relax in the moment, enjoy the activity, and let it unfold. Notice how it feels to simply let go,
   to stop trying to control everything, to be in the moment
   without a plan.

o Note your level of presence in varying situations. At work
   and home, note when it is easy or challenging. Which
   situations are more likely to keep you from being fully
   present?

o Note your reactions when life doesn't go as planned. What
   is your pattern in those moments? Are you fighting reality? Are you trying to control something over which you
   have no control?

CO-CREATIVE CONVERSATIONS

Creativity is contagious. Pass it on.

—ALBERT EINSTEIN

Possibility conversations come alive in dialogue with others. Using the right brain/left brain partnership as inspiration, we can explore the benefits of and barriers to collaborating and co-creating with others.

As we did in perspective conversations, we will explore the traps and tricks that make for more effective co-creative conversations. "Let's discuss" is a common way we talk about our interactions with others when we're trying to solve a problem, professional or personal. The word *discussion* has its roots in Old Latin from *dis* (apart) + *quatere* (to shake), similar to *concussion* and *percussion*, "to strike" or "to break apart." We think of discussions as ways to hammer out ideas in order to make a decision. As we learned in perspective conversations, if everyone comes to the table armed with their talking points, ready to defend their position and win, listening loses. Practicing open advocacy and inquiry helps us become better listeners and consider other perspectives, readying us for creative, open-minded explorations in conversation.

Dialogue, a distinct conversational tool, is a world apart from our typical conversations. David Bohm (1917–1992), a theoretical physicist, was a champion of this type of conversation. The word *dialogue* has its roots in the Greek words *dial* (through) and *logos* (word or meaning). Dialogue is a conversational process distinct from how we think about discussions. Dialogue asks us to consciously suspend our assumptions and judgments to allow a deeper listening. I have experienced by coaching others that nonjudgmental listening creates an emotionally safe space. A space where hard-fisted positions soften, more tolerant moods can surface, and creativity can magically bubble up. As we suspend our beliefs; expose our stories, emotions, and facts; and ask the four questions, our minds open up, seemingly impossibly disconnected dots connect, and unforeseen solutions rise up. While dialogue and open advocacy and inquiry are challenging, they are crucial steps for generating successful creative conversations. It's hard to put aside our biases and judgments, but at work and at home, the pleasure of co-creating is personally and collectively exciting.

Making music is an excellent example of the partnership between collaboration and co-creation. Experienced musicians play, listen, interact, blend, and sync up. Score or no score, plan or no plan, musicians co-create music whose whole is far greater than any of the individual parts. It looks and sounds so easy when that synchronization happens. While playing, musicians are present in the moment, listening to one another feeling the instrumentation, the dynamics, the tempo, and the mood. What looks effortless is in fact deep synchronicity—heads, ears, hearts, and hands creating a symphony of collaboration and co-creation.

How can we listen, collaborate, and create with the attention of musicians? How do we engage both the right and left hemispheres of the brain so we can successfully co-create? From stories to collaboration, we move from me-centric patterns of communication to inclusive patterns where we invite colleagues, direct reports, family members, and friends to have broad exploratory conversations. Of the four questions, authority plays a major role in silencing creative conversations. Claiming our voice or allowing other voices to be heard is the key to generating contagious inspiring co-creative conversations.

○ ○

After the retirement of Michael, the VP of the communication team of an auto company that I worked with, Rebecca, the VP of public affairs, was tapped to add the communication team to her portfolio. After a few months on the job, Rebecca had set new goals for the team but was frustrated and concerned about her new team. She was convinced that the team was capable, but she wasn't sure why they seemed so broken and lackluster. Her intuition told her that something wasn't right, so she asked me to sit down with the team without her to assess how they were doing. I agreed, but asked that my conversations with them to be confidential. I would report common themes and snapshots from the meeting. I wouldn't report any names or offer her direct quotes. She agreed and I invited the team to meet with me.

Here's a shortened version of that conversation, which included eight people:

Me: *Thanks for agreeing to meet today. Rebecca asked me to meet with you confidentially to get a sense of what you're thinking and feeling about the current state of the team.*

[Silence]

Me: *Here's what I mean by confidentiality: I will listen to your thoughts, feelings, and ideas and collect major themes from our dialogue. I will report back to Rebecca with those themes, an assessment of the team's current state, and a plan for making positive sustainable changes to meet her goals. No names or quotes, just ideas and a snapshot of where things are. I'll share my assessment with you and Rebecca. I want this to be a safe space where we can talk openly and honestly. Can someone start by stating a desire or concern that they have about where things stand?*

Barry: *I love this work, and we've been working hard this past year, but Michael has been tough on us. We're still reeling, and I suppose that's been obvious to Rebecca, but I am willing to work through this with her.*

Me: *Tough in what way?*

Terri: *We didn't seem to ever be able to please him. When we presented our work, he'd often dismiss our ideas and send us back to the drawing table. He wouldn't like the tone or concept of a media campaign, and he'd say things like, "No way can I show this to my colleagues. They'll eat me alive."*

Barry: *The funny thing is that in meetings, he'd also lash out at his colleagues, saying that they don't appreciate our work and don't have a clue what good communications can accomplish.*

Me: *So, how did you all respond to his behavior?*

Carol: *I tried several times to speak to him one on one to clarify what he expected or what his goals were for the next year. He said that their work was constantly a moving target, and we had to be fast on our feet and figure things out as we go. It was always about Michael. He never took responsibility and often complained about his colleagues or boss not trusting him to do his work.*

Terri: *This past year has been miserable. We each do our independent work—writing, creating social media campaigns, videos, etc. But Michael's tension always ran high, and our collaborative team spirit was at an all-time low.*

Me: *Sorry to hear all of this. I did get a feel for Michael's style when I worked with him last year. So here are some questions for you: What do you all want? What goals might you be able to agree on? What do you think of Rebecca's new gameplan?*

Terri: *I like her plan for the next year. But we also have to reset how we work together as a team.*

[Heads nod.]

Carol: *This is a tough job for Rebecca to take on. We all respect her, but we need to do a reset on our meetings and the team dynamics. With Michael we were desperately afraid to speak up for fear of having our heads chopped off publicly. I think we're still frozen by that fear.*

Me: *Okay, so I'm hearing that your ability to work and really shine as a team was at an all-time low. But you want to work together and you're willing to work with Rebecca toward a fresh start. Does that sound right?*

[Heads nod.]

Me: *Okay, then let's just go to the whiteboards and generate some ideas. What's possible? What team culture would make you a better team? How does your work intersect? How could you work together better? What kind of leadership would support you in doing your best work? What would a different tomorrow look like?*

Let's break up into two teams. Each team gets a whiteboard. First, I want you to talk about these questions as a group for twenty minutes. Second, I want you to answer each question by drawing a picture or a diagram of each question so we can see how they might fit together as a whole.

I gave each team lots of colored markers and started the clock. I heard lots of sighs.

Terri: *Just pictures?*

Me: *Yes, but this isn't a pretty picture contest. We all know how to draw a stick figure, mountain, and a sunrise. I want you to break out of your current thinking and wonder about what's possible. What would a future state look like that would make you a best-in-class communications team?*

As I watched the teams engage, the energy in the room slowly picked up, and after twenty minutes of dialogue, they got to drawing. The teams laughed as they drew pics and illustrations of fresh ideas.

After forty-five minutes, both teams had a diagram to share with the other team. The two teams went in different directions. One team drew their mission as an overarching rainbow, and their different functions were clouds below. Weighted lines showed how they were connected and also disconnected. The other team drew a winding road map as their next year's journey. Along the road were road signs like, "Work as a Team," "Have Meetings That Matter," "Safe Zone to Speak Up," "Stop, Ask Questions Before You Push Go," and "Back Each Other Up, Rebecca Included!"

Back together as a team, I asked them to synthesize the two versions of the future. That conversation was collaborative and creative. They combined the mission-driven, connect-the-dots diagram with the cultural ideas about how they could work better together. They were excited, and for the first time all year, they felt hopeful.

We then made a list of five things that they could do to move their new ideas forward.

1. Have a meeting with me and Rebecca to show their pictures and discuss their ideas.

2. Request a meeting with Rebecca to agree on their mission and on a strategy for the year.

3. Work with Rebecca to reset our team dynamics and agree on a few cultural norms.

4. Each director would create a new brief on their work and describe how they could better intersect with the other departments.

5. Work with Rebecca and me to rethink their meeting structure and cadence (dysfunctional meetings are one of my pet peeves).

6. Ask Rebecca to reintroduce the one-on-one meetings that Michael dropped.

The meeting was a great success. There was a lot of hard work ahead, but the ideas they generated were a great start to resetting their dysfunctional patterns and lifting their spirits.

As with the other conversations, the four questions guide us. What desires, concerns, authority issues, or standards have us locked down? Can we invite others to dialogue and explore nonobvious creative ideas? Can we eliminate power plays, find our voice, and invite all voices into a conversation to explore possibilities? In the unresolved conversations between Antonio and Jane and Robert and Allen, subtle power plays meant no one could speak their minds safely. Their conversations were stuck at the story level, never allowing them to advance to a collaborative—much less a creative—conversation.

In board rooms and living rooms, we need to recognize how authority issues—the root of discrimination, intolerance, and biases—loom large in the background of our disagreements and counterbalance unchecked authority by encouraging safe, open-minded, open-hearted, conversations.

Big Wheel, Little Wheel

Years ago, I worked with a senior executive of a car company, who, while walking to lunch, made a quip about one of their cars, wondering aloud, "What would a pink Riatta look like?" Months later, when his schedule took him to the secret design room, he was presented with a pink Riatta! The whole kit and caboodle: pink leather, pink tire walls, pink steering wheel, pink body. He was stunned. How had this happened? He hadn't asked for this. His innocent quip had taken on a life of its own. One decision led to another, and eventually his company had manufactured a single pink car. The executive named this phenomenon the "Big Wheel, Little Wheel" theory.

One leader (a.k.a. the big wheel) with lots of authority makes a sidebar comment, and then the next level of wheels start turning, and then the next and the next, until skilled workmen's tools were furiously spinning to make the pink parts. No one asked the leader a single question about his desire to see a pink car. No one thought to ask, "Are you serious about this? Would a drawing do? Could we build a model?" No one questioned his authority. The unquestioned authority silenced all voices at the cost of tens of thousands of dollars. A bundle of money would have been saved by asking the authority figure a few good questions.

In my example of moving to Boston to go to architectural school, I was torn by the many voices that said that my goal was impossible. The certainty of the relatives, colleagues, and friends who doubted me weighed on my decision. Fortunately for me, the strength of my intuition and the pull of the unknown outweighed those voices. Finding my voice was a valuable lesson in recognizing and claiming my personal power.

It's easy for a person with authority (e.g., a boss, parent, teacher, captain, coach) to believe their words are just one voice among many in the room. They think that they're simply stating their opinion or voicing their ideas like everyone else. But the more stripes we have, the more weight people give to our every word. In my work, I use the metaphor "the power of ten." In general, listeners/receivers of a message assigned ten times more significance to what is said by their leader. Most interactions are subject to this unconscious and unintentional consequence. As a parent, leader, or friend, it's easy to forget the weight of our words and our gestures. In my "not a big enough man" story, I heard the words and unconsciously assumed that they were true. As a consequence of the power of ten, opposing perspectives are silenced, inquiry doesn't feel safe, and creative possibilities are never considered. Any leader can practice embracing the inherent imbalance of the power of hierarchies and change their style to consciously encourage conversations with emotional safety. A culture of safety creates smarter teams and families.

Not long ago, Americans were mostly unconsciously living according to the authority, rules, and rituals of our local communities. The boundaries and standards of our communities were clear, and our shared morals were obvious. Right and wrong were well defined. These social norms have value, but as we slowly became a global community, we were exposed to differing ideas about equality, governance, education, marriage, religion, and so on. Because different communities hold different standards, it became less and less easy to stick with the story of our community.

The #MeToo movement is a perfect example of how cultural and social norms evolve. Men have been using their power to abuse women emotionally or sexually for millennia. This power dynamic was always unfair and toxic, but in most domains, the abuse went unchecked. As life evolved and cultural norms shifted, individuals and groups of people courageously spoke up, named names, and rejected old standards. We saw a significant shift in consciousness. Demeaning and humiliating patterns were rejected, and new norms and standards were crafted.

Technological advances are the twenty-first century's contribution to the evolution of human culture. Evolution is a packaged deal. As human consciousness evolves, there will be powerful reactions: fear-based refusals, rebuttals, and violence. For many, the unstoppable changes are very scary. *What will it mean for me? How do I keep information secure?* The most sensible response to these fears is being open to change and being fully awake to the benefits and dangers of new technologies. We can ask ourselves these questions: What new standards do we need to protect private citizens? How can we harness new technological advances that benefit our community? How is culture and society changing, and how do we influence and adapt?

In our homes, offices, and nations, as we learn to appreciate the contradictions and complexities of the world, we become participants in more conscious communities. Slowly, more and more people wake up, and cultural and social norms can be reset. It's a rocky road, but I'm hopeful that tolerant, open-minded, creative, and more-informed citizens will prevail.

Unlocking our creativity is a prerequisite for the next conversation: commitments.

PRACTICES

o Practice purposefully engaging in a conversation to explore possibilities at home or at work. Whatever the subject, give yourself permission to imagine beyond the boundaries of your current thinking. What other concerns, desires, or standards might help you explore beyond your story? In this process, pay particular attention to judgments that can quickly shut down new creative ideas.

o In a meeting or discussion note the center of your attention. Is your thinking self-centric? Experiment with consciously putting your attention on others to expand your thinking and creativity.

o Note situations at home and work where authority issues get in the way of exploring possibilities. Who is shutting down the conversation? What can you do to encourage creative conversations?

o What are your patterned reactions to change? With technology, decisions, or uncontrollable events, note your response and practice focusing on creative solutions.

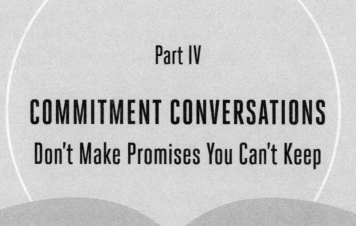

Part IV

COMMITMENT CONVERSATIONS
Don't Make Promises You Can't Keep

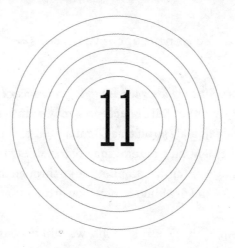

THE CONVERSATIONAL BYPASS

*Language sets everyone the same traps; it is an immense
network of easily accessible wrong turnings.*

—LUDWIG WITTGENSTEIN, Australian-British philosopher of mind and language

n this chapter, we take an in-depth look at the crucial role our everyday commitments play in our work and home lives. The daily promises
we make to ourselves and others, the agreements we sign, the time we
spend coordinating action—that all shapes our days, our plans, and our
future. We explore how our agreements work, how they fail, and how we
can recover from them when they go awry.

In the introduction, I wrote, "We live in conversations like fish live
in water." Commitment conversations are so much a part of our daily
routine that, without a second thought, we make promises on autopilot.
They come in the form of the obvious and subtle, the weighty and elementary. *I'm going to quit this damn job today. In the meeting this afternoon, we'll cover the budget without fail. If we agree, I'm ready to sign the*

agreement. Let's split the kids' pick-up today. I'll never trust him again. A commitment can either fail or succeed. I may or may not quit my job. The meeting could quickly go off track. I might not pick the kids up from school. The agreement may falter. I may regret not trusting him. With our commitments running on autopilot, we go through the motions with very mixed results and are blind to how powerfully they determine our collective lives.

With the help of the four questions, we will deconstruct the complexity of commitment conversations to better understand and navigate them. The commitments we make embody our desires, our issues with authority, and our spoken and unspoken concerns, and those commitments are the standards by which we measure success and how we create the future together.

We effortlessly nod in agreement, offer a handshake, give our word, and sign on the dotted line, at home and at work. And, voilà, we made a promise to coordinate action with others. We agree to complete the report on time, form a new partnership, quit our job, do the dishes, take out the garbage, make dinner plans, or lose fifteen pounds before the holidays. On autopilot, we agree to do things that we don't want to do, and we don't do other things that we agreed to do. We say, "Sure, no worries. I'll take care of it," or, "Okay, that's what we have to do," but at the same time, our private conversation is saying, *Damn, do I really have to do this?*

Coordinating action with others is the backbone of our relationships, companies, communities, and nations. The commitment conversation is primary to how we work, play, and build trust with one another. If I say, "Sure, I'll pay you $100 to edit my proposal," and you agree, our futures will be shaped by the outcome of that promise. And the $100 I pay you allows you to do something you might otherwise not have been able to do. The commitments we make and keep not only create an interconnected chain of coordinated action, they also determine our future.

At the heart of how we make or break commitments is nothing less than our personal integrity and trust. A kept promise tells us we can trust a person with whom we had an agreement. *Ah, Susan does great work. She's a keeper.* Or, *To my surprise, the kids actually got the job done on time. Next time I won't doubt them.*

Conversely, we have all experienced the pain and stress of an unfilled promise. *I needed that report by 9:00 A.M. this morning. This guy isn't going to cut it. He's hopeless.* Or, *I'm always doing more than my fair share. Screw her. She's taking advantage of me.* A broken promise sows distrust and marks the first move in a blame-and-shame game.

The other conversations have been building a foundation for executing this final conversation. As I said in the introduction, this is the action conversation. We are in business to work hard, get stuff done, and meet our goals. Outside of business, we build relationships by coordinating our efforts to take care of one another and to build our communities. The commitment conversation is a natural partner with the storytelling conversation. We love our stories and we love taking action. "I love this project. We are going to kill it." Or, "I think we've beat this horse to death. Let's make a decision and get to work."

But this comfy partnership between the two conversations has a major drawback. If we are convinced of our stories or if we fall victim to groupthink, overpowering voices, we can execute what I call the *conversational bypass*, which sounds something like this:

"Let's kick this into high gear."

"This has been dragging on for too long! I just want to get to it."

"Yeah, we've been down this rocky road before."

"Vineet isn't here. Let's start without him, he's held up with the boss. He'll go along with whatever we decide."

"This one's easy. We all agree on what the fix is, right?"

"Done. I'll work out the schedule and send it out tonight."

In this brief conversation, the participants, anxious to get to work, didn't consider other perspectives, possibilities, or solutions. They sailed from storytelling to commitment and assumed that they had it all figured out. At times, quick decisions are a must, but in this example, it turned out that Vineet had critical information that didn't surface for two weeks. The decision had to be revisited and two weeks' worth of work was useless. A little conscious effort and thirty minutes of time would have avoided a bad decision.

The "big wheel, little wheel" story from Chapter 10 is a good example of the conversational bypass. When Dave the boss asked, "I wonder what a pink Riatta would look like?" not one leader asked a single question or raised a concern. No one said, "Hey, Dave, how about we draw that up or make a model?" Why didn't they ask a question? Authority, the pressure of time, the absence of an environment that promotes open inquiry, and an addiction to action.

When on autopilot, we too often make quick promises and decisions and skip collaborative and creative conversations (see Figure 8). I have witnessed this rush to action countless times in business, family, and town meetings. The usual causes of the bypass are groupthink, big egos, extroverts overpowering introverts, and an imbalance of authority.

FIGURE 8: The conversational bypass

Bypassing the collaborative and creative conversations at work and home

○ Minimizes understanding.

○ Encourages hierarchical, imbalanced decision making.

○ Discourages listening.

○ Allows prejudgment and limits exploration.

○ Narrows the field of potential ideas.

○ Limits out-of-the-box exploration.

○ Maximizes quick, narrow decisions.

Being aware of the bypass and the purposeful execution of all four conversations is the first step. Asking the four questions is a good check to determine what might be rushing us into action. Unexplored desires can drive us to make quick judgments, our concerns can cause us to worry incessantly and rush to unnecessary action, a power imbalance can cause us to press for fast decisions, and our standards can narrow our thinking and limit our decisions.

I can't count how many times I have rushed to a decision while on autopilot. Sometimes those decisions are weighty, and sometimes they are inconsequential, but they consistently deliver unintended consequences. My desire to have that new shiny object outweighed rational considerations and I regretted the purchase two months later. My concerns about my son's wellbeing set me into action prematurely. My unexamined standards launched me on a judgmental rant about someone's service.

The bypass is an ingrained pattern that requires a conscious effort to avoid it. When I propose to teams that they take a few minutes to walk through a collaborative and creative conversation before making a decision, often they say, "Sounds good, but deadlines are looming." Notice how the left brain sneaks in there. We have little time. We have schedules to meet.

The decisions we make and the actions they set into motion are consequential. Teams or families that succumb to the bypass discover in time the ramifications of their ill-advised decisions. We have all jumped to a decision only to discover days later that the issue was not thoroughly vetted, that our thinking was not tested, or that we rushed a decision while we were emotionally triggered. How much time, money, and resources are required to redo a rushed decision? My position is that we can't afford not to take the time. I advise teams and families to spend the time to purposefully initiate collaborative and creative conversations to avoid rushed decisions.

The political arena is once again a great example of how calamitous the conversational bypass can be. In the halls of Congress, there is little understanding of or appreciation for collaborative and creative conversations. In their quest for power, many politicians don't consider compromise or the value of finding common ground. Much of the body politic has been hijacked by narrow positions. Grisly conversations full of mistruths and selfishness have displaced substantive conversations on issues that matter. Rather than focusing on dialogue and compromise, opposing tribes hammer one another's positions to prove their points and win the day. In divided politics, there's little or no interest in agreeing on the facts, productively discussing differences, or exploring ideas. Concerns are disregarded, standards are unbending, and critical problems go unresolved. Facts are shunned, and competition trumps compromise.

A good example of how entrenched positions halt progress is the decades-old conundrum of US immigration policies. We have plenty of facts about the issues. Research shows that undocumented immigrants make up roughly 3 percent of the population, and a considerable percentage of them are employed. But because emotions run high in this country, it's easy for many to ignore that fact. A number of positions that the right has taken up inject fear into the center of the conversation. Instead of relying on facts and lessons learned from the successes and failures of immigration history, populism and nationalism have hijacked the conversation. If only we could quarantine a group of congresspersons, senators, and a few experts to lay out the facts, explore the history, consider different options, and generate sustainable options. Imagine if we refused to let them out until they did their work!

Social cohesion and democracy are at risk when fake news, alternative facts, and bizarre conspiracy theories take Uncle Sam by the throat. This political insanity and dysfunction are fearful reactions to social change. I believe in these unsettling political times that rationality and tolerance will triumph. Since the Renaissance, we humans have been on a journey in which science and rationality have led us toward expanding and inclusive social norms. Facts matter. Science matters. Rationality partnered with intuition matters. Despite fearful slides backward, the overall human trajectory is upward, and scientific discoveries and increased consciousness of the world's interconnectedness leads the way. I'm an optimist, and I believe that rational thinking, scientific relevance, and conscious conversations will resurface to win the day.

Today, as I edit this manuscript, Vladimir Putin is indiscriminately bombing the people of Ukraine. Who could have imagined two weeks prior how dramatically his criminal actions would wake up the free world? The courage of the Ukrainians and the coordination of the actions of the free world is a reminder of how the evolution of consciousness will always vanquish evil. It might be a slow and painful journey, but conscious conversations and shared commitments can hasten our progress toward a better world.

Technology is also playing a significant role in the way that we connect and communicate worldwide. Global events are now available minute by minute for anyone with Internet access. Google, Facebook, Twitter, Instagram, and email allow anyone to connect with everyone, anywhere, in a flash. As with previous significant technical revolutions (e.g., the printing press, radio, and TV), the availability of advanced computers and technology are rapidly and dynamically affecting our societies. This revolution crosses physical, cultural, political, and financial boundaries. Because world news is accessible twenty-four/seven, we're on a one-way ride to a global community, which will have profound repercussions on our thinking and conversations. Climate change, pandemics, and economic inequities are pointers with a message. As the world gets smaller because of technology we will, in time, learn to have conversations that transcend borders. Business and religious leaders, teachers, and parents should aim to skip the bypass and purposefully engage in collaborative and creative conversation. Our decisions will be the wiser for it.

The best way to break the bypass habit is to better understand the intricacies of commitment conversations.

PRACTICES

○ In a meeting, see if you can catch people engaging in the conversational bypass unawares.

○ As a leader or participant, suggest that your group purposefully take time to share perspectives and engage in a collaborative conversation to create more understanding and clarity.

○ After a healthy collaborative conversation, purposefully shift gears and allow time for a creative dialogue. Observe the emergence of new ideas not previously on the table.

○ Note how voices of authority can create the conversational bypass. Depending on the situation, encourage leaders to minimize their influence, support multiple perspectives, and devote time to thinking about possibilities.

12

REQUESTS, OFFERS, AND PROMISES

Make small commitments and keep them.
Be a light, not a judge. Be a model, not a critic.
Be a part of the solution, not the problem.

—STEPHEN COVEY,
author of *The 7 Habits of Highly Effective People*

n the world of linguistics, there are five basic linguistic moves or speech acts. The storytelling conversation explores the first two of the five: facts and opinions. The other three are parts of commitment conversations: requests, offers, and promises.

Much like the dance of advocacy and inquiry, commitment conversations are a dance but with distinct steps:

1. When we want to coordinate action with others, we initiate the action with a request:

"Can you complete the report by Friday?"

"Would you work with me to whiteboard our new strategy?"

"Please sign the agreement as soon as possible."

Or an offer:

"I would like to facilitate the meeting."

"Let me handle the delivery of the bad news."

"I want to the make changes to the contract."

2. For every request or offer, we can give any one of these responses:

Yes

No

Counteroffer

3. When we say no, the dance ends. No agreement is made.

4. When we say yes, the dance begins. We have an agreement.

5. An agreement sets things into action to fulfill the promise.

Then we get to work, and life is good. What could go wrong? Well, this dance is trickier than we realize. Promises get broken for a myriad of reasons (e.g., misunderstandings, miscommunications, a lack of clarity, changed minds, and changes of heart). Life doesn't feel so grand when our colleague doesn't do their job, our boss unexpectedly ships us off to another department, or our kids lie to us.

Promises are a big part of everyday life, and they deserve more of our attention because our requests from others and offers to the world influence our next hour, day, and year. Making a commitment is an agreement to take on a responsibility and execute some action. They are nontrivial and autopilot won't do.

○ ○

Jacqui asks her administrative assistant, Fred, to gather images of a recent project for a critical presentation with the executive committee the following morning. She tells him the specific points she wants to make and the photos that are important. She asks for at least twenty-four different slides by 4:00 P.M. the same day. Fred asks a few questions about format and key concepts to make sure he understands. She answers his questions, and Fred gives her the thumbs-up, "I'll get it done."

Fred delivers thirty great pictures an hour ahead of schedule. After a quick review, Jacqui thanks Fred for a job well done. This was a successful commitment conversation, and neither Jacqui nor Fred gave it a second thought.

We check off so many items on our daily to-do list that each commitment seems inconsequential. When our promises go off without a hitch, they are effortless, a normal part of life. Until they aren't. A broken promise is a trigger for our noisy, angry, and disappointed private conversations. And we wonder, *How the hell did this go so off the rails?*

Let's replay the Jacqui and Fred story. In this version, Jacqui is late for her next meeting, and she zips by Fred's desk, letting him know that she needs slides today for a presentation the next morning. He looks up and gives a quick nod, and Jacqui heads off to her meeting. At 5:00 P.M., Jacqui starts to stress out. *Where are those slides? This isn't rocket science.*

When Fred finally emails the pictures at 7:00 P.M., Jacqui is spinning. Her private conversation isn't pretty. As she looks over the slides, her private thoughts are. *He's late, not good enough for the executive committee, wrong damn format, and not nearly enough images.* Frustrated that the job isn't complete, she knows she will have to work late to redo the slides and will have to change up her dinner plans. She's furious with Fred.

Meanwhile, Fred is having a great night pleased that he got the job done. He is unaware of Jacqui's harsh judgment or that he didn't fulfill a promise he made. Jacqui blames Fred, unaware that her hit-and-run request is in part responsible for the broken promise. She leaves the office stressed and ready for a drink.

Our Blinding Stories and the Background of Obviousness

The commitment conversation is especially susceptible to how our stories blind us. When we make requests and offers, they seem crystal clear and reasonable to us; we are unaware that our thinking, beliefs, and prejudices are embedded in every request and offer we make. Our story isn't their story, yet we assume that others are thinking like us. What seems obvious to us is not obvious to others. For Jacqui, the requirements for a good presentation were obvious—a high level overview for the executive committee, twenty-something slides, a bulleted format, and simple images with few words. If only Fred could have read her mind.

On a sunny Saturday years ago, I asked my sons for some help outside. They were playing with the fall leaves in the yard, and I told them that they could each earn five bucks if they raked the leaves while I did some errands. They were delighted to make a buck. I returned about an hour later, and the kids were smiling proudly, ready to be paid. From the looks of it (according to my standards), they had done a crappy job. They moved the leaves into many small, disorganized piles, and they didn't do the flowerbeds or the cellar wells. I was aggravated and disappointed, and I let them know what a lousy job they had done. They ended up in tears.

This seemingly straightforward request is an example of how obviousness can trip us up. It was obvious to me what a good job looked like. My standards were simple: I expected one big pile of leaves, and I wanted the flower beds and the basement wells cleaned up. I didn't have to think about what *good* looked like. I just *knew* it. They did the job as they saw fit. Here's the rub: my hastily made request caused the broken promise, but I accused them of not doing what they promised to do.

This dynamic plays out all too frequently when we coordinate action with others at work and at home. The commitment conversation dance moves at lightning speed. We make a request, hoping for a mind meld with others, then they say a quick okay, and we have made a promise that will most likely fail.

Figure 9 shows the whole dance.

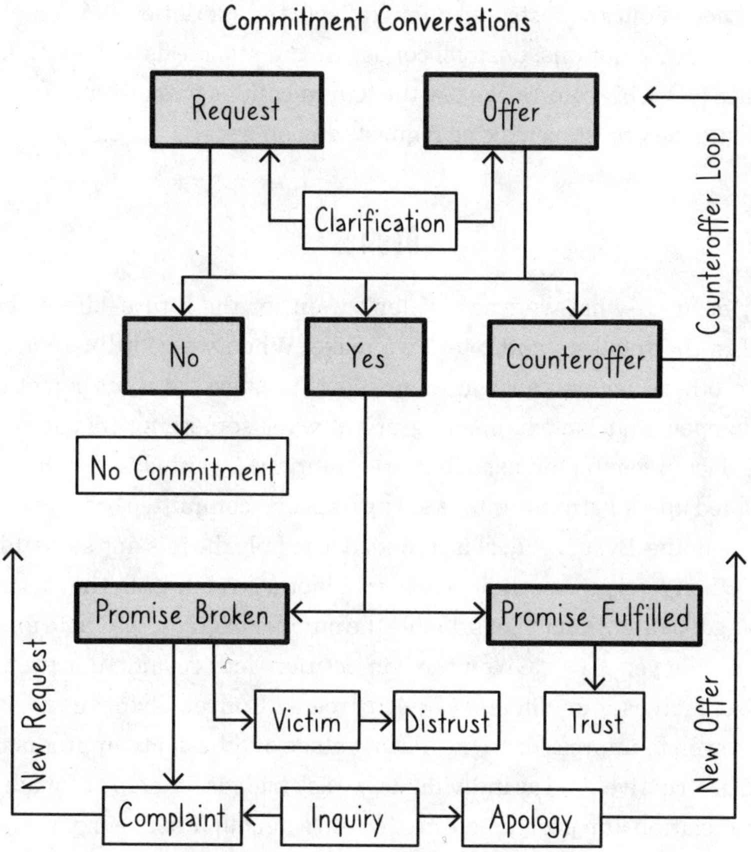

Commitment Conversations

FIGURE 9: Steps in the commitment conversation

Let's take a close look at each part in the dance.

Requests and Offers

We set events into motion when we ask for help, share information, offer an opinion, or make a decision. Whether by email, Zoom call, text, letter, or in person, the goals we want to achieve always start with a request or an offer (see Figure 9). "Can you edit this draft?" Or, "Would you like help downloading the files?" Or, "I want to run your campaign. How about it?"

Each of our requests and offers reflects the subtleties and complexities of our emotions, desires, concerns, and standards. And authority issues play a big role. So we use the four questions to more successfully execute the first step: making requests and offers.

Desires

Our desires—what we want or don't want for the future—are embedded in the requests and offers we make. When we coordinate action with others, we make requests or offers because we want something to happen that isn't happening or we want something that is missing. Jacqui wanted an excellent presentation. I wanted to get the yard cleaned up. Congress wants to set up a special committee to investigate wrongdoing. Every request is intended to supply the missing something.

When leaders ask their teams to adopt a stretch goal, they usually have good intentions. "Let's double the number of grants we write for the upcoming year." Or, "Given the competition, let's revamp our product line to increase our efficiency by 40 percent." Conversely, desires driven by power, to impress or to the disadvantage of others, are unproductive and destructive. And as individuals, we ask friends for help or for advice with relationship problems, offer to help a neighbor in need, or set New Year's resolutions. Or we make a request of ourselves. *I'm going to lose fifteen pounds by March.* Being mindful of our desires ensures that we make promises—from the practical to the inspirational—that can be fulfilled.

Concerns

When making a request or an offer, concerns are busy running in the background of our minds. They can be significant to our request, but obvious to us, so we forget to share them. When I asked the kids to rake the leaves, I didn't explain to them that rotting leaves can harm the grass and flowerbeds. When Jacqui asked Fred to put together the images, she didn't tell him her concerns about how to win over the executive committee.

Our concerns are a critical part of the success of our requests. If we are on the receiving end of a request, we can ask about specific concerns. "What concerns do you have about the presentation for the meeting?" Inquiry is a vital step toward making a solid commitment, thus averting many breakdowns.

Authority

Hierarchy and power play a significant role in commitment conversations. The example of Fred and Jacqui illustrates how hierarchy dynamics make for sloppy promises. As a leader or parent, we think we are making a simple request, but in hierarchies (both social and organizational), the decision-maker's request rings loud. In hierarchies, the boss is responsible for setting goals, establishing standards, and making decisions. Power dynamics are often responsible when requests are agreed to without question. We say things like, "No problem. I'll get right on it." Or, "Okay, that's a good idea." The influence of authority in this conversation, puts the responsibility on the requester to make a clear request. How a leader makes a request can slow things down enough to avert a quick "Sure, no problem." "Here's how I'm thinking about changing the process," the leader might say. "Let's take a few minutes to make sure we're on the same page."

In my family, it wasn't uncommon for my mother to ask my siblings and me to do something by saying, "Look at this mess! If it doesn't get cleaned up, your dad is going to be furious." She was invoking his power to get us to do something she wanted us to do. Similar dynamics play out in the business world. Managers sometimes make a dubious power-play request, invoking the boss upstairs. "We have to work this weekend to finish these numbers or Jennifer will have our hide." Or they make requests without revealing where it originated. "I want a report on our fourth quarter sales ready for Monday's board meeting." Or, "This new process has to be in place within six weeks." In both examples, it's not clear who made the original request, and that matters. Is it someone other than the person making the request? Was it a senior executive? Was it another team?

In my family, my mom leaned on my dad's authority to get what she wanted. This tactic might work in the short-term, but it's not sustainable. My siblings and I eventually figured out what my mom was up to. In the business examples, Jennifer, the boss, never asked the team to work over the weekend. The report on the sales numbers was a request by the CEO, and the six-month process change was based on a consultant's recommendations. The way that a team responds to a request and what they produce can vary depending on who has made the request. Understanding the origins of the request helps us avoid mistakes, which saves time and will more likely satisfy the requester.

Power dynamics also play out through our body language and our tone of voice. We can make a request in a variety of ways, from fair and humble to demanding and nerve-racking. And we can receive them as inviting and inspiring or harsh and judgmental. Fast, stormy requests set one mood, while thoughtful, clear requests set another. When a boss barks, "Have the outline for the board presentation on my desk tomorrow morning!" there's little room for questions. Such requests are more like demands that offer no safe way to say no. A more thoughtful, revealing request encourages inquiry and mutual understanding. "Can we compare our thoughts on the outline for the board presentation at 9:00 tomorrow morning?" Or, "I know we're both super busy, so how about we finalize the budget together this afternoon?"

When making requests, the opposite of abusing or mindfully using authority is not claiming our rightful power. When we feel unsure or insecure, we can make timid requests: "Do you think you could finish that report sometime soon?" "Maybe you can help out with Mom next week?" When we catch ourselves in this pattern, it's time to investigate our stories about authority. To whom do we give up our power? How, when, and with whom do we shy away from speaking up?

In general, our pattern is to make more requests than offers. Tomorrow, take note of the requests and the offers you make. While they are less prevalent, they aren't less relevant. Paying attention to how, when, and with whom we make offers can provide us with valuable insights. Questions like "What am I offering to this job, person, project?" or "Am I doing my best to offer my capabilities?" aren't common, and the words don't roll off the tongue. But when we investigate the offers we make or don't make, we might discover stories that limit our potential.

Recently, I was on a Zoom call with Gary, a high-profile engineering client; we discussed his one-on-one with his leader, Darrell. His strategy was to ask Darrell what he needed to do to be promoted to VP. What I heard in that request was his reticence to be clear about what he wanted and deserved. Gary is a very well-regarded engineer in his field and has had multiple exciting job offers from great companies in the last year, but his planned approach with Darrell was meek. I asked him to think about his desire to be a VP and to consider how that level of authority would help him achieve the company goals. His request to Darrell was missing the conviction that his engineering and leadership skills were being underutilized. As he reflected on his desires and value, he was able to turn a deferential request into a confident offer. This reframing of the conversation helped him present himself as a gifted talent. Busting a limiting story can help us rediscover all we have to offer to our work, our families, and our friends.

Standards

Our standards are also a silent player in how promises are made. We make requests, offers, and promises in the hope that our desires will be fulfilled. But how is that fulfillment measured and determined? Who makes the call? If all is fair, the determination that a promise is satisfied belongs to the requester. In fair play, a boss, a colleague, a friend, or a spouse has the authority to declare a promise fulfilled based on their standards. But, similar to concerns, our standards are so obvious to us that we fail to discuss and find agreement on them.

What does a good job look like? How are we going to measure our success? What determines completion? In construction, a building project comes with a tome of specifications that articulate quality and quantity standards for every part of the project. They cover everything from the quality of concrete to the style of doorknobs. In business, standards are also ubiquitous. How is performance measured? What rules of finances do we follow? How are stocks valued? What are the rules of hiring and firing? In an ideal world, the standard adopted should align with the goals of the enterprise. And our home life doesn't escape the consequences of standards. How much TV can the kids watch? What's a well-made bed? How much sex is enough? What's the proper mealtime? On and on! And the so-called softer skills of emotional and social intelligence depend on standards as well. How do we resolve conflict? Are white lies helpful or harmful? What are socially acceptable ways to say no?

Standards are usually inextricably linked to authority issues. Who makes the rules? Whose standards matter? Who determines if a commitment is fulfilled? I recently worked with an executive around the restructuring of the company into several divisions. With the restructuring, she was sure to acquire new leaders, and she was concerned about their ability to meet her standards and her ability to attract and hire upper-level external talent. As the leader of a new division, she had to have the authority to set the performance and cultural standards to fulfill the company's mission.

Time (A Subset of Standards)

The element of time is embedded in all requests or offers. Besides satisfying our desires based on standards, promises also determine that action "A" will be completed by person "B" in "X" amount of time. Time is a critical factor in every promise, small or large, fulfilled or broken. Like the other elements of the dance, we can make a promise, easily forgetting to address the timing required to declare the job done.

Based on our life experiences we have varied patterns with time, falling somewhere between hyper-punctual or perpetually late. Like many patterns and preferences, it's easy to forget that our interpretation is only one of many possible interpretations. When we make commitments, "ASAP" is a typical time-pattern default. It's convenient, but fuzzy. It could mean in the next hour, tomorrow, or next week. This makes our requests or offers sloppy. When we are triggered by our boss being constantly late for meetings or our partner holding us up, we can't believe how others can be so disrespectful or inconsiderate. Some leaders respect the time of their employees by starting meetings on time. Other over-scheduled or clueless leaders don't give their tardiness a second thought, oblivious to the impact it has on others. A party starting at 7:00 P.M. means one thing in some US cities and another in some Latin American countries.

I have no clue when, where, or why I adopted my time standards for being on time. But with my wife in the earlier example, or with a common problem of overbooked and overworked clients, I had to quiet my impatience and learn to resolve timing issues by agreeing on what "on time" means.

Clarifying Requests and Offers

The dance seems so simple. Someone makes a request or an offer, someone gives a response, and, voilà, a promise is made. We now know that a quick, "Sure, I can do that!" to our leader, colleagues, or friends is fraught with booby traps. The quick yes is a form of the conversational bypass. The benefit of slowing down the dance to ask clarifying questions helps us avoid the consequences of a broken promise. Clarifying a request or an offer adds a step to the dance: 2a. Before responding, we should slow down long enough to clarify the elements of a request or offer. Please refer back to Figure 9.

1. Every time we coordinate action with others, that effort will start with a request:

   "Can you complete the report by Friday?"

"Would you give me some of your time to whiteboard our new strategy?"

Or an offer:

"I would like to facilitate the meeting."

"Let me handle the delivery of the bad news."

2a. Prior to giving a response, we should ask clarifying questions to understand the elements of the request or offer.

2b. For every request or offer, we can give any one of these responses:

Yes

No

Counteroffer

3. When we say no, the dance ends. No agreement is made.

4. When we say yes, the dance continues. We have an agreement.

5. An agreement sets things into action to fulfill the promise.

Either the requester or the requestee can slow things down and ask a few key questions using the four questions as a guide. "Do you know who this presentation is being prepared for?" Or, "Can you tell me how the client will be using this information?" Or, "Would tomorrow work?" Or, "What format do you want?"

Taking a few minutes to understand a boss's perspective, a colleague's standards, or a loved one's needs increases the likelihood that we can make a mutually understood commitment. Then we move on to the next steps: our options for responding.

The next steps in the commitment conversation are limited. There are three basic steps: yes, no, and counteroffers. Refer back to Figure 9.

Yes

A quick yes to requests is easy, pleases others, takes little time, and can get things moving. An automatic yes in the form of a nod or a mumbled "sure" gets someone off our back, but it skips the clarification step (another kind of bypass), and it's a surefire way to sign on to a sloppy agreement.

For a leader, discouraging a fast yes is a great way to begin shifting the dynamics of the commitment conversation. If you are surrounded by yes-men (or women), you will be all too familiar with the bypass. Quick yeses are a sign that a company or a team needs to do more to create psychological safety and a culture that promotes the purposeful execution of collaborative and creative conversations.

A thoughtful yes is the better option. It creates breathing room in a conversation. Mindfully, we ask clarifying questions and consider the implications of the implied promise. Satisfied that we can fulfill the request, we can consciously choose yes with integrity and confidence.

No

Most people avoid no at all costs. Instead of easy and pleasing, it feels rude and contentious. But as one of my teachers, Rafael Echeveria, once said, "A request without a possible no is not a request. It is a demand." For that very reason no needs to be an acceptable option.

Power plays that discourage people from speaking up instill a fear of reprisal, rendering a no unsafe. Conversely, if we assign undue authority to others making requests, we can go silent, powerless to say no. No matter the cause, eliminating no as a legitimate option results in promises that we shouldn't have made, that we regret having made, or that we can't fulfill. To take care of ourselves or anyone else faced with unchecked authority, we must find the courage to say, "No, I can't do that for these reasons."

Over the years, I have discovered the power of saying no for myself. A few years ago, a CEO of a Fortune 200 company asked me to do a 360-degree assessment of a senior vice president. I had a fair amount of experience with the leadership team's struggle to work together. My intuitions were telling me to be cautious, but I agreed to do the 360. We agreed on goals, a process, and a schedule. After a week of confidential interviews, I gave my assessment to the CEO and the VP. The evaluation wasn't rosy and pointed to multiple issues related to the VP's leadership and communication styles and to strained relationships with his colleagues—hard news to deliver. The VP rejected the feedback. He was reluctant to move the process forward, and in the weeks that followed, he criticized the assessment to his CEO and doubted my work and effectiveness. My takeaway from that experience was that I needed to summon the courage to listen to my intuitions and learn to say no. Since then, I have turned down multiple requests when a leader wasn't ready to accept tough feedback, to do their work, or to grant me authority as their advisor or coach.

Counteroffer

A less-typical response to requests and offers is the undervalued and underappreciated counteroffer. Counteroffers are easily forgotten because of our patterned rush to yes.

When we take the time to clarify a request and understand it, we are better able to offer a fitting response. A simple yes might make sense and feel right, but it's more likely that we won't be able or willing to fulfill all the elements of the request. So, we can make a counteroffer (see Figure 9). We could offer that a diagram might work better than bullet points, an interim review, a different timeline, or a different goal. Clarifying questions and counteroffers aren't obnoxious when their intent is to gather missing information and create mutual understanding to create a promise that will be more likely to be fulfilled. In Fred's case, if he had asked a few clarifying questions, he would have discovered a surprising amount of information. With that information, he would have had a new appreciation of the scope of work and he could have made a counteroffer asking for an extra hour to be sure he got it right.

Another type of counteroffer is to ask the person making the request for time to consider their request. "Could I please have a few hours to research the data so I can nail this thing?" We might need a few hours or a day to collect information and consider priorities and schedules before committing to the request. A thoughtful counteroffer takes both parties back to the beginning of the dance. (Please refer back to Figure 9.) We can loop from request to counteroffer and back to request/offer and back to counteroffer until there's mutual understanding of the promise.

Fred's counteroffer is actually a request, "Can I have an extra hour to pull it together?" and Jacqui gets to say yes, to say no, or to make a counteroffer (see Figure 9). She can counter by saying, "How about 5:30 when I'm free?" If Fred says, "Yup, that works," then they have made a new agreement that is more likely to be satisfied in the future.

I learned to make counteroffers before saying no. On two other occasions when leaders asked me for an evaluation/assessment, I countered by requesting a signed agreement with the persons involved with the process (rules of the game). My counteroffer ensured that the leaders were aware of my standards, the process, and the organization's goals for the consultation. A successful assessment included a commitment to acknowledging and working with the feedback I would give them. They also had to commit to doing the required work to change their behavior and the perceptions of their leadership. Those two experiences had quite different outcomes. One leader wouldn't accept the guidelines of the process, much less acknowledge that she had work to do. I decline to continue with the work. Calamity avoided! The other leader fully embraced the process and recognized that he had some work to do, so I signed on, and we embarked on a six-month journey that served him well.

o o

In hierarchies and families, how we engage in commitment conversations—the responses we make, can't make, or don't make and the promises we make or break—have major repercussions for ourselves, our relationships, and our work. This conversation syncs up all the tools we have learned in the other conversations. Making requests, asking clarifying questions, and making counteroffers are forms of collaborative and creative conversations. Open advocacy and inquiry, mutual learning, and the humble exploration of ideas will always produce better promises and more trusting relationships.

The importance of commitment conversations is a humble reminder of this adage: The one constant in the world is change. Life regularly delivers unexpected slips and slides, and in spite of our best efforts and our best-laid plans, promises break. In the next chapter, we will consider how to recover from broken promises by making thoughtful complaints and apologies.

PRACTICES

○ Notice the nature of your requests. Are they casual, vague, or demanding? Does the style of your requests change in the various domains of life? Using the four questions, how would you improve your requests?

○ Take note of your body signals and intuitions when making or receiving requests. Is your intuition telling you, *My gut isn't feeling this* or, *My instincts are telling me this isn't okay*?

○ Take note of the quantity of your requests and offers. Most people make more requests than offers. How are your requests and offers different if you make them in the context of family, friends, or work? What was your last offer? To whom did you make the offer?

○ Offers also reflect the stories we hold about what we can and can't do in the world. Reflect on stories that could be limiting how you think about yourself. In what domains of life could you make a bigger, more daring offer?

○ What's your pattern of responding to requests and offers? Does your pattern include the auto yes? How would it feel to ask a few questions for clarity before agreeing to a request? Experiment with counteroffers. Notice how that changes how you coordinate action with others.

○ Reflect on a few unfulfilled commitments. Use the four questions to uncover what went wrong. Was the promise sloppy? Were there any power issues at play? Are there times when you don't feel safe to make a counteroffer or to say no?

13

RECOVERY CONVERSATIONS

*People won't have time for you if you are
always angry or complaining.*

—STEPHEN HAWKING

n spite of our best efforts and intentions, we never know how things will play out because the unexpected happens. The estimates were wrong, the team leader quit, the kids got sick, a storm took out our power, or minds changed. Broken promises trigger us, and when we are angry and complain about or blame others, we are playing the victim, and we spiral down to the bottom of the funnel rather than summoning the courage to understand how and why a promise fell apart.

Promises are broken for reasonable, innocent, and malevolent reasons. A broken promise could be the result of an anxious yes, forgetfulness, changed circumstances, an act of nature, insincerity, or simply bad luck. It could be as simple as a continuously late boss wasting employees' time, or a devastating situation involving a loved one breaking a promise that breaks the bond of a relationship. Some make insincere promises with spiteful intentions, but most people make promises with good intentions. For the most part, breakdowns are a result of sloppy promises and misunderstandings. When promises fail, individuals and relationships suffer, plans and projects falter, and trust erodes.

As individuals, the ways that we react to a broken promise are telling. Are we blaming others without taking responsibility? *Why didn't they hold up their part of the deal? Did they miscommunicate? I did my part.* How do we respond when we make a mistake? *Did I misunderstand what she wanted? What can I do to repair the damage done?*

In relationships, every broken promise generates consequences. *Why did he agree to an interview and then not show up? Did something happen that prevented her from picking up the kids? When I made this promise, was I aware of the expectations and standards?* It's natural to respond to these situations with automatic anger and negative judgments. But knowing the complications of this conversation, we have the tools and can explore what went wrong. Every promise is complex, so open inquiry is once again the go-to tool.

Broken promises also slow progress on our work. I have seen projects and goals stalled for months due to unfulfilled promises and distrust. We know too well that there are no winners in the blame-and-shame game. Our egos rear their heads, and we become defensive. We are convinced that our story is right and that the other person is simply deluded. Then we spiral down, bitching and moaning all the way. Our private conversations are full of toxic thoughts like, *I'm not getting thrown under the bus for this! I'm telling the board this is your fault!* Or, *It's not my fault! Someone else is purposely making us look bad.* Pointing fingers and holding on to self-righteous stories can feel good, but the negative consequences are significant. Unresolved broken promises break friendships, marriages, partnerships, and projects.

One finance company I consulted for asked me to attend an offsite retreat, where the tax team and the finance team weren't talking to one another. Worse yet, the teams were openly criticizing each other across the company. By the time I entered the scene, the friction between the teams was intense. Misunderstandings, broken promises, and distrust had become the norm for the team's interactions, and they didn't know how to collaborate and to integrate their work.

After setting rules and goals for our days together, we began a round robin, and each person—with no interruptions—had one to two minutes to say what they wanted to get from the retreat. The intent of the round robin was to surface varying perspectives. When we were finished, I broke each team into smaller groups and asked them to list or diagram their grievances. I specifically asked them to use the four questions as a guide to present their feelings, thoughts, and concerns with an open hand. After about thirty minutes, the subgroups reported back to the whole. As each group told its story, I encouraged others to ask questions to promote understanding. This group conversation was the first time the teams had been able to hear one another. Here's a snapshot of some of the things they said: "Did you guys really think we were trying to sabotage your work?" "I had no idea that your major goal was around acquisitions or new business opportunities." "I don't understand the standards and laws you guys are concerned about." "I'm concerned about some of the behavior of a few of your team members. Whatever we do here has to apply to our teams."

Both teams were highly frustrated because they believed the other team was setting up obstacles and slowing down the decision-making process. The finance team thought that the tax team provided super conservative tax advice and constantly set up roadblocks to exciting new business opportunities. The tax team felt that the finance team was offering business proposals that were too risky for the company.

There was plenty of time during the offsite for the teams to socialize. A fishing expedition, skeet shooting, and other activities helped the team members connect personally. Fun and laughter are always a good antidote for toxic tension.

When we got back to work, I had the two teams diagram what a different integrated collaborative future could look like. The teams' reportouts were remarkably similar, and after a few hours of dialogue, we started documenting actions to reset their relationships. They agreed to set up a cross-functional sub-team to map out an integration plan. They created a few cross-functional quarterly meetings to stay connected, share info, and collaborate to solve any crossfire. The teams also established a few cultural and process norms to work together more successfully (e.g., attending a social breakfast or after-work event, establishing inquiry as the default to avoid misunderstandings, adopting collaboration when mutually beneficial, speaking up and giving one another constructive feedback, and creating a process map to detail how cross-functional decisions would be made).

In our final exercise, each leader reflected on and wrote down three things they wanted to do differently in the future. At the close of the meeting, each leader shared two of their ideas. Some leaders committed to being better listeners before jumping to conclusions. Others wanted to model and to share with their teams the agreements from the offsite. A lightbulb went off in the heads of a few, who then committed to changing their aggressive communication style. It took several days, but the tension-filled room gave way to open hands, minds, and hearts and to a chance to rebuild trust, which is earned over time, conversation by conversation, action by action, commitment by commitment. Its foundation is built on solid agreements, kept promises, and the successful execution of those agreements.

The foundation of distrust is the result of multiple promises gone awry. A story of distrust is destructive. Thinking, *I don't trust him,* isn't trivial, and giving that feedback is scary. We avoid these tough contentious conversations, but that doesn't resolve or changes the circumstances and it's a disservice to ourselves and to others. Rather than avoiding or getting stuck in a pattern of blame and shame, we can deconstruct trust to better understand and address it.

Three elements constitute trust:

Competence: Is incompetence an issue?

Sincerity: Were both parties to the promise sincere?

Reliability: Is reliability a recurring issue?

Competence is a commonly forgotten yet crucial element of trust. When making a request, we easily forget to consider if we or others have the skills, knowledge, and experience to satisfy it. Our patterned rush to rush skips the opportunity to assess competence. Before committing, it is better to admit up front that we need time to learn a skill or check if others are competent to get the job done. No blame, no shame. Making a new commitment can present opportunities for teaching and/or learning.

Sincerity is an assessment of the difference between what someone says they will do and what they deliver. Conscious or unconscious, insincere behavior can reveal unresolved authority issues. Do we keep steam rolling over others because we are afraid to admit a mistake? Are we unconsciously afraid and unable keep a promise? Are we saying one thing while thinking and doing something else (private conversations)? Are we on autopilot, saying yes to a new plan while hoping the project gets sabotaged?

Reliability is about our standards of quality, quantity, and time. Do we finish the job according to the agreed-upon expectations? Do we deliver when we promise? Did we discuss clear standards when we made the promise? Did we show up when we agreed to?

The tax and finance teams came to the offsite full of distrust. The finance team considered the tax team insincere and unreliable. Rather than doing their jobs, they tried to expand their power by putting up roadblocks for the finance team's projects. The tax team considered the finance team incompetent, and believed their proposed projects were putting the company's reputation and security at risk. As the teams discovered how divisive their lack of trust was, they shared their thoughts about competence, sincerity, and reliability. They had a new shared language to better understand and rebuild trust.

The Walk-Away Option

When we inquire into the reasons a request went wrong, we can assess responsibility, power, psychological safety, and trust issues. If we determine that a request isn't worthy, we can consciously choose not to engage with the other party, aware of the potential consequences of walking away for the individuals, relationships, and the task at hand.

Last year, I bowed out of an online group conversation centered around politics. In spite of my best efforts, the others wouldn't discuss facts or consider other perspectives. When I asked them to send me the sources that supported their claims, it was clear that they had fallen down a rabbit hole of conspiracies, misinformation, and lies. When I shared my facts and resources, the group rejected my facts out of hand as the "MSP," or the "main street press." I cared about and worked with some of the group members, so I made my case for sane conversations, then I let them know that I'd no longer participate in the group. I was free of the stressful interactions and never looked back.

A famous Zen koan asks, "What is the sound of one hand clapping?" I like to ask my clients what a one-way conversation sounds like. What do we do if we enter a conversation with an open hand and heart but we meet a fist? If we determine that a conversation is unsafe, if it involves unfair power issues, if the parties won't use facts as a foundation, if minds and hearts are closed, or if statements are rooted in uninformed ignorance, we can choose to say no and disengage from a conversation. A one-way conversation isn't worth our energy.

Inquiries, Thoughtful Complaints, and Apologies

The final elements of commitment conversations are thoughtful complaints (a promise that someone else broke) or apologies (a promise that we broke). See Figure 9 in Chapter 12.

When we conjure up the courage and curiosity to investigate a broken promise, we are moving to the top of the spiral, open to facts, life-changing events, miscommunications, and a possible sloppy promise. Thoughtful complaints and apologies are collaborative and creative by their nature. We explore what happened, right wrongs, and find ourselves back to the first step of the commitment conversation, ready to restart the dance.

Thoughtful Complaints

A *thoughtful complaint* (as opposed to a mean-spirited one) is a sincere attempt to understand how and why a promise was broken and to check in with others to understand what happened. In making a thoughtful complaint, we might discover that we made a sloppy promise, and together we might recover and start fresh. We might also discover that the other person didn't live up to their end of the bargain, agree on the damage done, and make a request to repair that damage.

Remember the case of Fred and Jacqui: imagine if Fred had been two hours late in delivering the pics. Jacqui could have taken a breath and asked a simple question to clarify the promise: "Didn't we agree on 4:00 this afternoon?" But that's easier said than done. To do that, we have to unhook from our emotional reactions (e.g., frustration, anger, disappointment) to inquire without blame or judgment. A thoughtful complaint starts at the very beginning of the commitment dance. What was requested? What was promised? Were we on the same page for timing, quality, and results?

If Jacqui had asked, "Didn't we agree on 4:00 this afternoon?" and Fred said, "I'm so sorry, but I got lost in the year-end numbers," or he might reply, "I put 5:00 A.M. on my calendar. Sounds like I blew it." In trusting relationships, we can react with curiosity, empathy, surprise, or amusement.

With everyday promises, it's usually easy to let things slide. Why make a fuss? But that's exactly how sloppy promises are perpetuated— missed deadlines and unclear expectations prevail. Without thoughtfully and humbly addressing these breakdowns in real time, they recede into the background and become fodder for future misunderstandings.

When we take the time to understand why a promise was broken, we inquire, listen to the other's response, adjust our thinking, and assess the damage to ourselves, our relationships, and our tasks. Processing our private conversations can come in handy. Jacqui's private conversation sounded like this: *I just can't trust this guy! He hasn't been reliable three times. I can't afford to give him another chance.* By investigating her private conversation with the four questions, she could have assessed the breakdown, determined what when wrong, and made a thoughtful complaint. But if she doesn't investigate the broken promise, trust between them will erode, and the same mistakes will reoccur.

A thoughtful complaint is complete when a new request is made (see Figure 9 in Chapter 12), and the dance begins again. To move on and avoid future breakdowns with Fred, Jacqui could have made two requests: "Okay, Fred, but in the future, let's agree to take a few minutes to make sure we're on the same page about my requests. If I do a fly-by, slow me down or text me your questions. And since I'm under the gun today, I'd like to spend an hour in the morning together to update the presentation." If Fred agrees to both requests, then a new commitment is made and they can rebuild their trust.

Some broken promises are more serious. The boss doesn't keep his word. Someone runs a red light and demolishes your car. Your partner doesn't show up as promised for dinner. The kids get home three hours after curfew. While these carry a heavier emotional load, they require the same investigatory effort. In most situations, no matter how triggering, we can take a breath, slow down, move into inquiry, assess the breakdown, and start anew with a request for reparation.

A Thoughtful Apology

A thoughtful apology also begins with a sincere attempt to understand how and why a promise was broken and to check in with others to determine what happened. We might discover that we made a sloppy promise and mutually decide how to recover and start anew. We might also discover that we didn't live up to our end of the bargain.

A humble apology is our best option when we realize and accept that we are responsible for a broken promise. To do that, we must unhook from embarrassment or blame and explore just what went wrong. A thoughtful apology revisits the promise. *What did I promise? What did I not deliver? Was there a misunderstanding?* We might also consider the elements of trust, competence, sincerity, and reliability; then we can humbly accept responsibility for an agreement gone awry.

A thoughtful apology is complete when the person making the apology offers to repair the damage (see Figure 9 in Chapter 12). The commitment between Fred and Jacqui could play out differently. Fred may realize his mistake, and before Jacqui has a chance to complain, he might offer a thoughtful apology that acknowledges his perspective and that signals that he's willing to discuss what went wrong. "I realize that I wrote down the wrong time, and I know you have to be fully prepared for today's presentation. I'll get the pics in your draft presentation in the next two hours, and then we can review it together to make it perfect."

This is a far cry from an automatic "I'm sorry." *Sorry* has its place, but without taking the time to investigate why a promise was broken, it can be a whitewash to avoid conflict. With a thoughtful complaint, we assess the damage to individuals, relationships, or tasks, and we seek understanding. Then we can offer or ask for ideas about what we can do to take care of the damage. By exploring the breakdown, we might also discover that the other person took our actions personally, and we can offer assurance that our sloppiness doesn't reflect on them.

A humble apology (see Figure 9 in Chapter 12) leads us back to the beginning of commitment conversations. Our acknowledgment of fault and willingness to repair any damage invites a respectful conversation whose intent is building trust.

Time Spent vs. Time Lost

Many of us are time-crunched just trying to make it through another day, and it is easy to forget the steps required to make strong promises. They can feel complicated and time-consuming. As action addicts, we tell our stories, do the bypass dance, and race to get the job done.

Even at our busiest, we can benefit from a few minutes of thought so we can make more conscious commitments. Teams that endlessly blame each other and mindlessly execute the conversational bypass can spin for weeks and make costly mistakes. In families where members can't speak up, can't make themselves heard, or don't feel psychologically safe, misunderstandings and disrespect rule.

These final steps of recovering from broken promises move us away from well-worn patterns of defensiveness and guilt, and they complete our understanding of commitment conversations. With an appreciation of the complexity of a promise, we can slow down the dance, make clear requests and offers, and be mindful when we say yes or no or when we make a counteroffer. When necessary, we can revisit a broken commitment and make thoughtful complaints and apologies.

During the first three conversations, we expand our thinking, extend our radar to absorb other perspectives, and widen our search for ideas. The commitment conversation concludes by closing this expansion cycle with a decision, "Yes, we have a plan." We now have a new story to tell, "Here's the strategy. Let's get things moving." And with that, we restart the cycle of investigating, collaborating, and creating because the world will surely change around us. Well-executed commitment conversations are challenging, but when they are done well, they are a game-changer.

PRACTICES

o Take note of situations in which your response is defensive and you blame others on autopilot. What fears might be lurking behind that defensiveness?

o If things don't go as planned, when do you show up as the victim? Note how that restricts your ability to step back and understand why a promise was broken so you can appropriately apologize or complain.

o Reflect on a relationship where trust is in question. Deconstruct your story of distrust into the three components of competence, reliability, and sincerity. How could you use that information to invite the other person to a conversation to rebuild trust?

o Practice making a humble complaint. When another person doesn't fulfill a commitment to you, take time to ensure that the promise was specific and clear. If the initial promise was unclear, perhaps a complaint isn't appropriate. If it was clear, invite the other person to agree or not on what happened on their side. Use the four questions to help reveal and understand the breakdown and the damage. Did they lose track of time? Did they not know how to do the job? Whatever the breakdown, acknowledge it, then make a request to repair the damage and to avoid a similar mistake in the future.

o Think about a past commitment that you didn't keep. Was the promise clear? If yes, use the four questions to explore why you broke the promise. Then use what you discovered to make a humble apology, explaining what happened and why. Complete the apology by making an offer to repair the damage.

CONCLUSION

A Lifelong Journey

How did the rose ever open its heart
And give to this world all of its beauty?
It felt the encouragement of light against its being,
Otherwise we all remain too frightened.

—HAFIZ, Persian mystic and poet

n the introduction, I promised to show the reader how to engage in better conversations. I hope that over the course of your reading of this book you have noticed a shift in yourself and that you are newly attuned to nuances in conversations. If you have, then chances are good that you have become a better observer of yourself and that you are learning to minimize your inner critic, increase your empathy, and sharpen your sense of humor. Each small effort we make toward having more conscious conversations helps us be thoughtful, curious, and kind to ourselves and others.

Awake in Conversations

The four conversations are interconnected, and our everyday interactions flow and co-mingle, creating an intricate tapestry that continuously shapes our family, social, and work lives. In difficult moments, it's wise to move through the conversations purposefully—stories to collaboration to creativity—until we arrive at commitments. If you have caught yourself on autopilot, investigated and shifted a pattern or two, and invited others to collaborate and cocreate, then you are a more enlightened conversationalist.

Here are some of the ways that conscious conversations better our lives:

- Shifting old stories in our heads allows us to change our thoughts and reactions, hearing anew those we love and bringing our best selves to our work.

- Managing our emotional reactions helps us open our minds and hearts, and it improves our ability to engage with others. We can become more vulnerable, open to different perspectives, and able to enjoy unexpected collaborations.

- When we inquire about others' opinions, we discover and appreciate diversity of opinions and the freedom of not knowing. Collaboratively, we can rethink our standards, create shared goals, manage authority issues, and accept and unearth new possibilities.

- Giving ourselves permission to relax and wonder, we stand in awe of the mysteries of life. We practice not having all the answers and trusting our gut. And we appreciate the interconnectedness of ourselves and the larger context.

- Conscious commitments slow us down, which helps us make wise decisions. They avoid the conversational bypass and create trusting relationships. Being conscious of how we coordinate action with others will always improve the job at hand.

Our everyday conversations can be our teachers. Any interaction can wake us up to a harmful or nonproductive pattern. It's important to find an appropriate individual pace to practice the tools of the different conversations. Practice increases emotional intelligence, reduces limiting fears, renews faith in our gut instincts, and cultivates more attentive relationships. Despite our unique personalities and patterns, we all share a natural desire for living with less stress and greater wellbeing.

Engaging in conscious conversations is a lifelong journey. Even after thirty years of practice, I still have to keep working. On any given day, an event can wake me up and demand my attention. Life is messy, and in spite of our best efforts, the universe never tires of throwing obstacles in our way. Our practice won't change that, but they can change how we respond to the messy or the unexpected. Any shift we make, small or large, will help us unwind, relax, accept, and embrace life as it comes.

Be a Good Observer

Be a good observer of yourself and others. When we adopt a nonjudgmental attitude and a sense of humor, we can see our adopted patterns, beliefs, standards, and desires, all of which are promoted by the ego's identity. The four questions are our crib sheet for investigating our patterns and undoing ourselves mid-spin. They help us ask ourselves questions like these: *What's worrying me? Am I in a power struggle? Am I holding on to desires that are at odds with reality? Am I holding onto standards that drive me or others crazy? What feels different as I move up the spiral?*

As we become better observers and more aware of our stories, we are no longer stuck in them. As witnesses we are better equipped to investigate and change them. We can also accept that each person is an expression of their remarkable history and their particular stories. We each have our fair share of flaws, and we can appreciate that we are all doing the best we can at any given moment. Slowly, we can exorcise a few demons and become a little lighter, kinder, happier, and wiser.

Accept Reality as It Is

As we expand our awareness, we come to appreciate the larger forces of life. No matter what we call our higher being—God, the Prime Mover, the mystery (my favorite), universal energy, or life force—every aspect of our lives is integral to the larger mystery, the force of life embodied through us individually and collectively.

Our egos fool us into thinking that we are masters of the universe. If we don't investigate our stories, we can easily fall into the trap of believing that the world revolves around us, then events trigger us, and we suffer. As we wake up, disappointing life events can remind us that life's complexities and interconnections are constantly in play. We will inevitably encounter dark forces, patterns of human belief or action that have unfortunate consequences. Some people are violent, intolerant, racist, or misogynistic. These are unconscious humans who believe the bizarre and who act in foolish ways. If we can learn to accept this reality—which isn't to say that we should like it—then we can engage and act in the world from a saner standpoint.

We are evolving patterns of human consciousness. We live on a (spiral) spectrum (see *Spiral Dynamics: Mastering Values, Leadership and Change* by Don Edward Beck and Christopher C. Cowan, based on the emergent cyclical theory of Clare W. Graves), which ranges from fear-based, self-centric behavior to an expanded, peaceful, and tolerant consciousness; from narrow perspectives of right and wrong thinking to acceptance of multiple ways of being and creative collaborations; from authoritative, top-down arrogance to mutual empowerment and enlightenment.

Acceptance of life as it unfolds expands our minds, aligns us with reality, and moves us up the spiral of consciousness. We will always dislike certain aspects of life, but kicking and screaming about injustice, inequality, screwy politics, stupid bosses, or even the weather keeps stuck on autopilot. Through conscious conversations, we can move from fighting reality to productively cocreating solutions, moving human consciousness forward and up the spiral. Here's how the four conversations can help:

The Storytelling Conversation: Your Stories Are Not the Truth

Enjoy your emotions and stories, but when they send you spinning, it's time to investigate. Tough love and laughter are required. Deconstruct each toxic judgment using the four questions. Bust the stories that limit what you're offering to the world. Undo old, restrictive self-assessments and adopt new stories that are true to who you are or want to be. Humbly admit to others that your stories are an interesting mix of biases, judgments, emotions, facts, and opinions.

The Collaborative Conversation: Seek to Understand and Absorb Other Perspectives

Open advocacy and inquiry are critical tools. Use the four questions to lay out your positions and to ask honest questions of others. Curious questions are your best way to absorb and listen. When we practice open advocacy and inquiry, we listen to ourselves and others with less judgment. We begin to see and feel their suffering, and we cultivate curiosity, openness, mutual understanding, and tolerance. These qualities move us up the spiral and greatly reduce our fear and anger. Daily practice yields small successes that have a powerful cumulative effect.

As good observers, we will notice universal patterns. We will see how we humans suffer in similar ways. As Henry Wadsworth Longfellow said, "If we could read the secret history of our enemies, we should find in each man's life sorrow and suffering enough to disarm all hostility." Understanding and compassion move us up the spiral toward a love that is universal.

The Creative Conversation: Trust Your Intuition

Before jumping into action or forcing an answer:

1. Experiment with slowing down, taking a breath, and permitting yourself to imagine beyond the boundaries of your story.

2. Take the time to collaborate and explore different perspectives and unexpected possibilities.

3. Always avoid the conversational bypass and the rush to action.

4. Lighten up, experiment, and accept that you can never have all the answers.

Our rational mind's job is to acquire answers, but when we ask curious questions, we broaden our thinking, see the world through a wider lens, and gradually learn to trust our gut instincts. When we let go of being right and being in control, we encounter a natural wisdom. We enjoy the moments of flow when we let go and when life unfolds in unexpected ways, then we get better at observing and accepting what we can and can't change, at embracing what we can and can't control. When our intuition is unleashed, we are likely to be more awake for whatever comes our way.

The Commitment Conversation: Don't Make Commitments You Can't Keep

As we become more aware of conversations, we quietly discover that we know what to do. We know how to seek clarity, when to say yes, when to make counteroffers, and when to say no. Rather than making arrogant demands, we humbly and respectfully make requests and offers that create better promises and yield more successful outcomes. And we know when to walk away from conflict to protect ourselves. As we undo stories that are holding us back, we can recognize when opportunities are knocking and more fully embrace the gifts and talents we have to offer the world. We can serve others by making conscious commitments that create successful and fulfilling futures.

If only we had a pill that would magically transform conversations to our liking. Minus the magic pill, we can choose the concepts in this book that feel right for us to practice. They will be with us for life and part of our journey. I have been practicing, succeeding, and failing for thirty years. There is no perfect way, but trying to do and be better, being present, open, and vulnerable in conversation is inviting, attractive, and contagious. Having more conscious conversations can help each day be less stressful, more peaceful, and rewarding. Each small step we take will ripple out into the world.

Enjoy the journey!

REFERENCES

Websites and Podcasts

Katie, Byron. "Whose Business Are You In?" Accessed April 19, 2022. https://thework.com/2006/09/whose-business-are-you-minding.

Lewis, Michael. *Against the Rules* [podcast], Season 2, Pushkin, https://pushkin.fm/show/against-the-rules-with-michael-lewis/.

Book References

Barrett, Lisa Feldman. *How Emotions Are Made: The Secret Life of the Brain.* Boston: Houghton Mifflin Harcourt, 2017.

Beck, Don Edward, and Christopher C. Cowan. *Spiral Dynamics: Mastering Values, Leadership, and Change.* Hoboken, NJ: Wiley-Blackwell, 2005.

Covey, Stephen R. *The 7 Habits of Highly Effective People.* New York: Free Press, 2004.

Goleman, Daniel. *Emotional Intelligence.* New York: Penguin Random House, 1995.

Kross, Ethan. *Chatter: The Voice in Our Head, Why It Matters, and How to Harness It.* New York: Crown, 2022.

McGilchrist, Iain. *The Master and His Emissary: The Divided Brain and the Making of the Western World.* New Haven: Yale University Press, 2010.

Pink, Daniel H. *A Whole New Mind: Why Right-Brainers Will Rule the Future.* New York: Riverhead Books, 2005.

Ruiz, Don Miguel. *The Four Agreements: A Practical Guide to Personal Freedom.* San Rafael, CA: Amber Allen Publishing, 1997.

Senge, Peter M. *The Fifth Discipline: The Art and Practice of The Learning Organization.* New York: Doubleday, 1990.

Tolle, Eckart. *The Power of Now: A Guide to Spiritual Enlightenment.* Navado, CA: New World Library, 1999.

ACKNOWLEDGMENTS

This book has been on my mind for twenty years and writing it has been more challenging and rewarding than I ever imagined. As I started, stumbled, stopped, and restarted, the support and encouragement I got from my family, friends, teachers, and clients shored me up to stay the course.

My career-changing adventure (with two young kids to feed and grow) and the writing of this book would not have been possible without my best friend, editor, and wife, Kata. In her quiet and kind way, she always supported me to move forward through struggles and doubts.

Little did my two sons Ben and Sam know that when they were growing up, they were convenient guinea pigs for me to experiment on with my new language knowledge. We would take walks in Harvard Square, and when I would start skipping, they would get very agitated and say, "Dad stop skipping; you're embarrassing us!" I would reply, "Who's embarrassing you? I am just skipping." They have grown up to be talented and kind men. Thank you for hanging in there with mom and me. Love you to pieces.

To my siblings, in-laws, and extended family, thank you for putting up with my many unsolicited proclamations about life. Your love, friendship, and sense of humor are invaluable.

Much of this book would not have been possible without my clients. A few gems who have supported my work over the last thirty years are Dave Meador, Peter Oleksiak, Doug Field, Jamie Bonini, Shawn Patterson, Steve Ambrose, Kathy Fellows, and Dave Fulkerson. To

them and all my other clients (no more names for fear of missing someone), your individual dedication to becoming better leaders and people
inspired me and many others. The world is a better place because of
your leadership.

To my friends, my talented and crazy bandmates, old friends in Cambridge, the crew in Wayland, and our tribe in Manchester, to name a
few—our comic to philosophical conversations are priceless. You all keep
me grounded and always wanting more. Thanks for putting up with me.

I could not have sustained the challenges of writing this book without the help of talented editors. Colleen Gillard, Jeannine Thibodeau,
and Peter Heyrman helped me with very early drafts. Morellen Macleash
worked with me for over a year and was instrumental in helping me
clarify, organize, and structure the concepts in the book that became
the foundation of this manuscript. I was also blessed to be introduced to
Maureen O'Brien by a dear friend, Joy Horowitz. Maureen is an accom-
plished editorial professional in the publishing industry. She was my
teacher as a "writer in training"; her coaching and encouragement kept
me in the game. And this past year, Jeremy Elvis Herman has been an
invaluable partner in helping me land the final manuscript. He is appre-
ciative, talented, and a kind critic.

Tom Miller of Liza Dawson Associates is my literary agent. Tom has
a strong record of handling bestsellers and award-winning books, and I
was thrilled when he showed interest in mine. To this day, I remember
our first meeting in New York. We had a good conversation, and he was
enthusiastic about the book. At the end he asked me what I wanted; I
said, "I want an agent to rep my book." He said, "Well, let that be me!" I
returned to my hotel room and shed a few tears of joy. Tom is smart, talented, experienced, tough, and a great advocate. Thank you for making
me and the book part of your portfolio.

With Tom's help, I landed a publishing deal with Berrett-Koehler.
Neal Mallet, my editor at Berrett-Koehler, has been encouraging. I can't
express how reassuring it was to have a veteran editor like Neal believe
in your manuscript. New to the game, I needed to be educated and stew-
arded through the complex world of book publishing. The whole team at

Berrett-Koehler has been professional and, given the nature of my book, their collaborative and co-creative mission is a perfect match. Hats off to all.

And finally, I want to give gratitude to teachers and colleagues who supported me over the last thirty years. Early in my career transition, I was fortunate to be trained as a Hellerwork body/mind therapist by world-class practitioners, notably Joseph Heller, Stuart Bell, and Don St. John. As I made my way into the world of advising leaders and teams, Linda Reid (who inspired me to pursue this work), Julio Olalla, Rafael Echeverria, Lesley Pollitt, Fred Kofman, Amy Fox, Devra Fradin, Verne Myers, Gary Morse, and Peter Axelson and the whole gang at Garnett Consulting were mentors and friends.

I have been counseled spiritually by Osho, Ramesh Balsekar, Wayne Liquorman, Byron Katie, Eckart Tolle, and Miguel Ruiz, to name a few. Their wise words resonate throughout the book.

INDEX

ABOUT THE AUTHOR

Chuck has spent thirty years as a trusted advisor, coach, and teacher in communication, human dynamics, and leadership excellence. He has worked with leaders and their teams in high-profile companies across industries. His methods are anchored in leading-edge research, theoretical development, and his expertise in conversations.

Our conversations reveal our individuality, the quality of our relationships, and our work and home cultures. His work is deceptively simple—he advocates for paying attention to conversations with fresh eyes, which holds the key to transforming ourselves and our collaborations, creativity, and decision-making.

Chuck has a degree in architecture from the Boston Architectural College and was a partner at HKT Architects in Cambridge, MA. He loved architecture, but several life events called him to change careers at the young age of forty. Chuck was among the first to be certified by the Newfield Group, a leading transformational education organization, as a professional ontological coach. He also trained in mediation and worked as a senior mediator affiliated with the Harvard Mediation Program at the Harvard Law School, and later, associated with MIT's Center for Organizational Learning, was a consultant in organizational learning, leadership, and culture.

Chuck has recently worked as an advisor and coach with leaders and teams at Google, Apple, DTE Energy, Ford Motor Company, and Tesla (all Fortune 200 companies). His client list has also included the Harvard Business School, PSEG, Peabody Essex Museum, Brigham and Women's Hospital, General Motors, and Chrysler Motor Company.

He lives in New England with his wife, Kata, an artist. They have two sons who are living out their creative dreams in New York City.

Dear reader,

Thank you for picking up this book and welcome to the worldwide BK community! You're joining a special group of people who have come together to create positive change in their lives, organizations, and communities.

What's BK all about?

Our mission is to connect people and ideas to create a world that works for all.

Why? Our communities, organizations, and lives get bogged down by old paradigms of self-interest, exclusion, hierarchy, and privilege. But we believe that can change. That's why we seek the leading experts on these challenges—and share their actionable ideas with you.

A welcome gift

To help you get started, we'd like to offer you a **free copy** of one of our bestselling ebooks:

www.bkconnection.com/welcome

When you claim your **free ebook**, you'll also be subscribed to our blog.

Our freshest insights

Access the best new tools and ideas for leaders at all levels on our blog at ideas.bkconnection.com.

Sincerely,

Your friends at Berrett-Koehler

Certified

Corporation